Alexander

Joseph & Emma Smith's Far West Son

EDITED BY RONALD E. ROMIG

John Whitmer Books

Independence, Missouri

2010

For Alexander

Alexander: Joseph & Emma Smith's Far West Son
Edited by Ronald E. Romig
Copy edited by Lavina Fielding Anderson
Cover, interior design, and maps by John C. Hamer

Thanks to Joy Goodwin for the image of Emma crossing the Mississippi River; Roland Sarratt, Church of Christ (Temple Lot) Church Historian, for furnishing an image of Leon Gould; Gracia Jones, Alexander and Elizabeth Smith descendant, for providing information about and photographs of members of the Alexander H. Smith family; Bob Wallace for researching the location of Alexander's home at Andover, Harrison County, Missouri; Community of Christ Liberty Hall, Lamoni, Iowa, for providing images of Emma Smith Bidamon and Lewis Bidamon; Buddy Youngreen, for photographs of Elizabeth and Alexander H. Smith; and the LDS Church History Library for pictures of Quincy, Illinois, Brigham Young, and the Young residence in Salt Lake City.

Published by John Whitmer Books, Independence, Missouri
JohnWhitmerBooks.com
Published in the United States of America
Copyright © 2010 by Ronald E. Romig
rromig@cofchrist.org

ISBN 978-1-934901-26-7

Table *of* Contents

Introduction

Alexander H. Smith, 1900s.

ALEXANDER H. SMITH'S heritage uniquely impacted his identity. The fact that Alexander's father, Joseph Smith Jr., was the founder of the religious movement known as Mormonism, bestowed rather distinctive status upon his family.

Born at Far West, Missouri, much of Alexander's life was devoted to providing ministry throughout America's Far West.

This pictorial biography employs excerpts of Alexander's personal writings, observations by his daughter, Vida E. Smith, and visual materials that highlight the life of this remarkable individual.

Emma Hale Smith

Emma Hale Smith oil portrait.
(Dixon, Illinois: Inez A. Kennedy,
Publisher, 1893), 96.

ALEXANDER'S mother, the former Emma Hale of Harmony, Pennsylvania, came from a line of refined, "well-to do" pioneers of excellent and strong character.

—Inez A. Kennedy, *Recollections of the Pioneers of Lee County*

Emma Smith's ring.

Joseph Smith Jr.

Joseph Smith Jr. oil portrait.

ALEXANDER'S FATHER was Joseph Smith Jr., the Mormon prophet. Alexander was born in the Smith home at Far West, Missouri, in June 1838.

Right: Joseph and Emma Smith's house, Far West, Missouri, 1838.

Born *at* Far West, Missouri

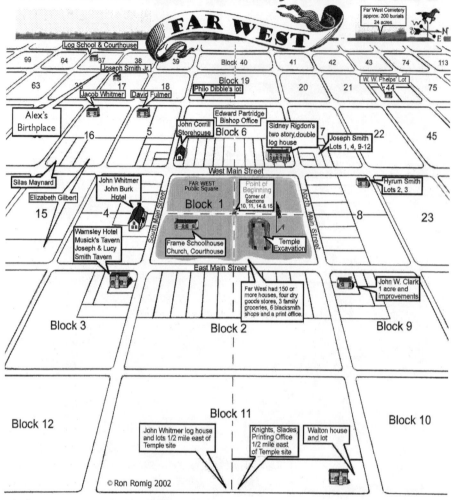

Alexander's birth location is shown on the map at top left.

ALEX WAS BORN ON June 2, 1838, at Far West, Missouri, on the western frontier, Joseph and Emma's fifth son and sixth child. Joseph Smith recorded the occasion in his journal, noting, "I returned [from a surveying expedition] on the first of June on account of my family for I had a son born unto me."

—June 1, 1838, *History of the Church of Jesus Christ of Latter-day Saints* (Salt Lake City, UT: Deseret Book Company, 1978), 3:37.

Namesake

Joseph Smith, 1830; Alexander W. Doniphan, 1840s; Emma Smith, 1842.

JOSEPH AND EMMA Smith named their son after Alexander W. Doniphan, their trusted family friend and lawyer. Alex's name also honors his mother's family, Hale. Alex inherited his father's "blue eyes and ruddy complexion." Joseph Smith's granddaughter Mary Audentia Smith Anderson observed:

Alexander had "a gentle and genial nature, instantly winning the friendship and confidence of those who knew him." Old time saints . . . [testified that Alexander] inherited a striking resemblance to his father in voice, gesture, and manner of presentation in the pulpit.

—Vida E. Smith, "Biography of Patriarch Alexander Hale Smith," *Journal of History* 4, no. 1 (January 1911): 5, (hereafter cited as "Biography of Patriarch Alexander Hale Smith," by date and page).

Expulsion *from* Missouri

CHURCH DIFFICULTIES resulted in his father's incarceration in the Liberty, Missouri, jail while Alexander was still an infant.

During a sermon at age sixty-three, Alexander reflected upon his early memories:

I could not give you a comprehension of the condition that surrounded me at my birth. . . . At the time that I speak of, the Church was in great difficulty; my father was taken prisoner and thrown into jail. My mother carried me, an infant, with her to visit her husband in jail. And from this time until I arrived at the year of my majority, the influences around me were of such a character that enabled me to feel that with no choice of my own, I had inherited what the world looked upon as a heritage of shame. . . . For at that time my father was looked upon as an impostor, and was persecuted

Liberty Jail, Liberty, Missouri.

Refuge *in* Illinois

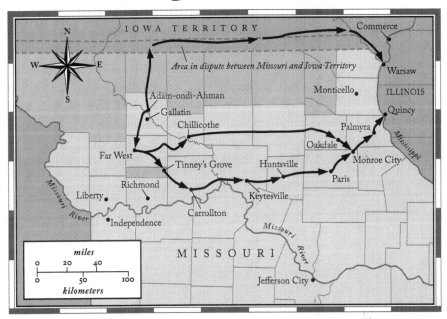

Mormon exodus routes from Far West, Missouri, to Illinois. Cartography by John Hamer.

and driven from city to city, and wherever his name was mentioned it was looked upon by the people as a synonym of evil, of wrong.

—Alexander H. Smith, "My Heritage," Sermon, Kaukura, Tahiti, November 10, 1901, *Vision* No. 53 (July 2006) 19.

In February 1839, Alexander's mother Emma made her way across Missouri to the shores of the Mississippi. Mrs. Smith crossed the river on foot, with her small son Frederick and baby **Alexander in her arms, and little son Joseph and adopted daughter Julia clinging to her dress.**

Emma crossing the Mississippi River. Courtesy of Joy Goodwin.

Cleveland Home *at* Quincy

City of Quincy, Illinois, photo by George Edward Anderson, 1907, retouched.
Courtesy the LDS Church History Library.

THE FAMILY FOUND temporary shelter from its foes on the friendlier shores of Quincy, Illinois, at the home of John and Sarah Cleveland. Alexander's antics provided a pleasant diversion as the exiled family helped the infant learn to walk around the Cleveland house. Emma fondly wrote to Joseph that Alexander was "so strong that with the assistance of a chair he will run all round the room."

—Emma Smith, Letter to Joseph Smith, March 7, 1839, Joseph Smith letterbooks, Ms 155, box 2, folder 2, LDS Church History Library.

Alexander H. Smith, age 5.

Nauvoo, Illinois

Hugh White blockhouse at Commerce, Illinois, as it appeared later, retouched.

AFTER JOSEPH SMITH'S escape from jail in Missouri in April 1839, the family moved to Commerce, Illinois, later known as Nauvoo. Joseph purchased an old but strong blockhouse from Hugh White for the family's home.

Here the family celebrated Alexander's first birthday.

Strawberries were in season and Emma often made strawberry shortcake for Alex's birthday.

Death *of* Alexander's Father

Joseph Smith Jr.

Hyrum Smith.

WHEN ALEXANDER was only a child of six, his father and uncle, Hyrum Smith, were killed while incarcerated in the Carthage Jail, at Carthage, Illinois.

Carthage Jail, Carthage, Illinois.

Emma *and* Brigham

Gold rings like those belonging to Hyrum and Don Carlos Smith.

Emma Smith, 1845.

Brigham Young, 1853.

FOLLOWING JOSEPH'S death, a profound and unfortunate animosity developed between Brigham Young and Emma Smith at Nauvoo. Alex recalled:

I had just turned my sixth year. And it would be supposed that the members of the Church . . . would have rallied around the stricken wife and mother of the President of the Church. But . . . my mother refused to attend their meetings and mingle with them. The officers of the Church recognized this and sent the teachers to her, that they might labor with her and have her attend the meetings, and let the influence of her presence be with them. She told the teachers that they were introducing and teaching things in the Church that the Prophet never taught, and she could not recognize them, neither would she lend her influence, by her presence, in their meetings. From this time there was an antagonism between the body known as the Church and my mother.

Brigham accused Emma of taking . . . rings from Hyrum [Smith]'s and Don Carlos Smith's widows and never returning them."
—Brigham Young, Jr., re: Emma Smith, April 1, 1867, Photostat, Emma Smith Papers, P4, f38, Community of Christ Archives (hereafter cited CofC Archives.)

William Marks, Nauvoo Stake President

EMMA ATTEMPTED to influence the selection of her husband's successor. She quietly supported William Marks believing that he, as Nauvoo Stake president, was the appropriate individual to lead the church instead of Brigham Young. This position resulted in continuing enmity between Emma and emerging church leaders. Ultimately, Emma's efforts on behalf of Marks proved unsuccessful. From that point on, Emma and her family remained aloof from gestures by the Twelve as they consolidated power.

Valeen Avery and Linda Newell observed that Emma's and Brigham's "mutual inability to resolve their differences cemented the divisions of the Latter-day Saints."

—Valeen Tippets Avery and Linda King Newell, "The Lion and the Lady: Brigham Young and Emma Smith," *Utah Historical Quarterly* 48, no. 1 (Winter 1980):

Battle of Nauvoo

&

Lewis Bidamon

Lewis Crum Bidamon. Courtesy Liberty Hall, Lamoni, Iowa.

IN THE FALL OF 1846, for the safety of her family during the Battle of Nauvoo, Emma moved to Fulton City, Illinois, 140 miles up the Mississippi. However, during the spring of 1847 the family returned to the Nauvoo Mansion House.

—"Biography of Patriarch Alexander Hale Smith," (January 1911) 12.

Alexander spent the remainder of his youth at Nauvoo, either living in the "Mansion," which his mother conducted as a hotel, at the Homestead, or on the family farm a few miles southeast of Nauvoo.

ON DECEMBER 23, 1847, Emma Smith married Major Lewis Bidamon, who was one of the first "new" residents occupying Nauvoo after the Mormon exodus. This union provided protection for Emma's young family and her property. In 1849, when news of the discovery of gold in California reached Nauvoo, Lewis went to the gold fields. Late in 1850 Bidamon returned to Nauvoo without any gold.

Nauvoo Temple

Weather vane from Navuoo Temple architectural drawings.

ALEXANDER GREW UP in the shadow of the Nauvoo Temple. As a youth, he had free access to the remarkable structure. In 1897, Alex recalled a memorable experience when he was drafted as a tour guide.

When a boy [about nine years old] I was privileged to wander all over the building, and sometimes when the man in charge did not feel like climbing up the many flights of stairs, which led into the cupola to show visitors the wonderful building and beautiful view to be had from the dome, he requested me to show them. I well remember that on one of those occasions I ventured out of the small door on the east side of the rounded top which was covered with bright tin. I walked all around it, and as I approached the door the gentleman whom I was guide to caught me and drew me in, and lectured me for my imprudence, declaring that he would not dare do it.

The offices in the corner to the left of main entrance on the ground floor were finished, but not furnished. The auditorium or main meeting room was temporarily finished; the seats and pulpit were only temporary.

The upper auditorium; the plastering was not done, the floor was only the rough boards, intended only for the lining, was laid, and from this floor upward the stairs, except in the tower, or circular main stairs, were also temporary; the upper floor which was to have been divided into numerous rooms was laid, and partitioned off with cotton factory cloth, and used for some purposes before the saints were driven away. I was told that the cloth of those partitions was subsequently used for wagon covers, by the saints on their journey across the plains.

To my knowledge the temple never was finished, and those who have been led to believe it was have been deceived.

—Alexander H. Smith, quoted in Heman C. Smith, "The Nauvoo Temple," *Journal of History* 3, no. 2 (April 1910): 161-62.

Nauvoo Temple tower.

Lucy Mack Smith

Lucy Mack Smith.

Lucy Smith

Painting of Lucy Mack Smith, by an unidentified Utah artist, based on Frederick Piercy's 1853 engraving. Courtesy L. Tom Perry Special Collections, Harold B. Lee Library, Brigham Young University, Provo, Utah.

DURING HIS YOUTH, Alexander's grandmother Lucy became a resident of the family home. He no doubt had many precious memories of Lucy but unfortunately did not preserve them in writing. Lucy died in 1856, while Alex was in his late teens.

Alexander's Gold Rush

Alexander H. Smith, 1859.

JUST LIKE HIS stepfather, young Alexander was also impacted by the allure of gold. When he turned nineteen, a new discovery of gold ignited a wild rush for Pike's Peak. Alexander

joined a party starting for that promising field. . . . [but did not get far] on this gold hunt [when] . . . the party turned back from the plains of western Kansas.

—"Biography of Patriarch Alexander Hale Smith," (January 1911) 12.

Alexander was also mechanically inclined and skilled at wood carving. Alex received a general education in the Nauvoo common schools. His mother's generous ways were a model of hospitality for him, while his stepfather, Lewis, schooled him in the arts of farming and husbandry. Alex did not appear religiously inclined as a youth.

Alexander proved to be good with horses and a good shot with a gun. Joseph Smith III related the following story as a witness of Alexander's' youthful prowess:

Mr. Lard ... another man named Thomas Jones, and my brother Alexander were the three best riflemen in the town. In those days shooting at a mark for pastime—or for turkeys or beeves—was a popular sport throughout the country. There was another man named Samuel Grotts, who lived out a way, who was also an excellent marksman, and between these four there was great rivalry. Though the youngest of the quartet, Alexander gradually outclassed the others and came to be considered absolutely the best shot in the county. It finally resulted in the master of ceremonies at the different shooting matches within a radius of twenty miles, when announcing the terms of the contests, winding up with the statement, "Open to all comers except Alexander Smith!"

—Richard P. Howard, ed., *Memoirs of President Joseph Smith (1832-1914)* (Independence, MO: Herald Publishing House, 1979), 169.

Alex's Family

The Bidamon-Smith family. (Left portrait): Emma. (Center portait left to right): Lewis, David, Frederick, Alexander, and Joseph. (Right portrait): Julia.

IN ADDITION TO a positive relationship with his mother and step-father, Alexander enjoyed a warm affection with his brothers and step sister Julia.

Alexander and David.

Marriage

EMMA BEFRIENDED a widow named Elizabeth Kendall whose family spent much time at the Mansion House. When Mrs. Kendall died, Emma made room in the Smith household for her eight-year-old daughter, Elizabeth A. Kendall, until she grew to womanhood.

Over the years, Alex's and Elizabeth's relationship grew more serious. They married June 23, 1861, ages 22 and 19, respectively.

The newlyweds moved onto the Smith family farm in Sonora Township. Their first child, Frederick A., named after Alex's brother, Frederick Granger Williams Smith, was born at the farm.

Alex's wife, Elizabeth A. Kendall Smith. Courtesy Gracia Jones and Smith Family Associaiton.

Alexander Smith.

Frederick Granger Williams Smith

Frederick's death was particularly hard on Alex and left him concerned for his brother's spiritual well-being. Alexander reported an early spiritual experience in which heard the whisper of the Comforter's spirit tell him, "Grieve not; Frederick's condition is pleasant; and the time shall come when baptism can be secured to him."

—"Biography of Patriarch Alexander Hale Smith," (January 1911) 14.

ALEXANDER'S brother, Frederick G. W., married in 1857 and started a family. But Fred's health failed in 1862 and he died.

Painting by David H. Smith symbolizing their dead brother.

Move *to the* Nauvoo Mansion House

Nauvoo Mansion House ca. 1880s.

Emma, sketch by David H. Smith.

THE HEALTH OF Alexander's wife Elizabeth became critical after Frederick A.'s birth, so Alex moved his family back into the Nauvoo Mansion House where Emma successfully nursed Elizabeth back to health.

—"Biography of Patriarch Alexander Hale Smith," (January 1911) 13.

A Hunting Story

Alex.

FOR A TIME Alexander tried his hand as a partner in a photographic gallery, then supported his young family by doing carpentry work and hunting.

Alexander excelled at all outdoor crafts. The following story, in his own words, conveys his great love of the adventure of the wild.

One evening, when a young man, I arose from my seat beside the fire, for the cool weather made a fire necessary to comfort, and passed to the door, and looked out; my wife noticed that I as restless and uneasy and remarked, "What is the matter with you?"

Now, that the reader may the better catch the thread of this little story, I will say I was then a young man of about twenty-four. Was married and lived in the Old Mansion, situated on the brow of the hill on the east bank of the broad Mississippi, whose beautiful waters shone in the light of the afternoon sun with enticings strong for me, for I dearly loved the old river. My wife saw the spirit of unrest was upon me, and was uneasy, because she and our baby boy had ere this been left alone for days, while I was off on the river, or in the woods, no one knowing exactly where nor at what time I would return.

Our brown eyed, dark haired baby boy was a joy to her, and a comfort when I was gone, but her heart was always filled with fear when she knew I was on the waters, or when I was gone and she knew not where. I was a good enough sort, had few bad habits, but unfortunately for my wife's peace of mind,

I was descended from a great hunter, only two removes [Emma's father, Isaac Hale], and in my blood was the taint;—a love for my gun and rod—and as the seasons for hunting or fishing came round, my blood became fevered with a longing for the woods, or river and lakes, and I could seldom resist the "call of the wild;" and so my wife many times found herself alone with our baby for days. With this explanation, the reader can understand with what uneasiness she asked the question, "Now what is the matter with you?" She had heard the call of the quail that afternoon, and knew that I also had heard it. Three separate times I left my seat and went to the door and listened. At last I sprang to my feet, caught down my gun, and say-

ing, "I'm going to see if I can find those quail; I'll not be gone long," I passed out, crossed the road, and was soon out of sight in the neighboring fields.

Now when I started out with my gun, I really had no thought of going beyond that neighboring field; but the spell was on me, and I could no more be content to abide in the four walls of a house than could the little martins stay when the time to go had come. In the first field I did not find the quail, so in the next I must needs go. I knew that the evening meal would soon be ready, but little cared I, while the impulse to roam was upon me. My footsteps soon led me past the dwelling of a neighbor, one Sam Chambers, whose love for a gun and the fields was as great as my own. As I approached the dwelling, I shouted and Sam came out, and as soon as he saw that I had my gun, he said, "Wait a minute and I'll go with you." Now Sam was a married man, too, and had a family, but the hunting nature was strong in him also; so, when he joined me, his blood was fired by the same fever and unrest that made me reckless of time.

When he came, he said, "Where to now?" I replied, "Oh, anywhere; let us go up the river." So up the river we went. Field after field was passed through, until just before the sun

Elizabeth Kendall Smith and Frederick A.

reached the horizon, we found our-selves some three miles and a half away from home and near the river bank. Then I remembered I had a canoe which had been left, still a half mile above where we were. The proposition was made to go and get the canoe and ride home. It suited both, and we were soon in the frail vessel speeding towards home.

The canoe was a small one, bare-ly able to bear up two full grown men, and when we were seated and had pushed off from the shore it ap-peared that but two or three inches of the gunwale was above water; but both of us were expert boatmen, and used to that kind of vessel, so we felt no fear. The weather had been cold several nights before, and ice had formed in the river north of us, and was now floating quite thickly in midstream. As we pulled out into the stream, some wild ducks flew past and settled in the water near the opposite shore. The river here was nearly a mile wide, and to reach the opposite side we hunters had to pass through the floating ice. But as it seemed very little out of our way, we at once proposed to run across and try for some ducks. True, by this time the sun was disappearing, but we did not mind that, as the evenings were light, as a rule, long after sunset; but unfortunately for us, as we neared the farther shore,

a fierce squall, or gale of wind sud-denly arose, and swept over the river, and our frail craft would not live ten minutes, in such weather, so we hastily sought shelter on shore. With the wind, came clouds and rain. The wind blew so fiercely it would catch up the water from the top of the waves and blow it in great sheets through the air. The night settled down in earnest and it be-came very dark. We were in for a night's stay on an island. So long as the wind raged, there was no escape. To add to our discomfort, we began to get very hungry, but there was no show for supper on that bleak is-land; no human habitation within miles and miles of us.

Through the island, which was large, some miles in extent, ran deep out narrow sloughs; the landing had been made near one of these.

I remembered a deserted woodchopper's cabin, a mile or such a matter across the island, on the banks of this water way, and I proposed to take to the boat and keep close under the bank, and if possible reach the old hut for shelter for the night; and now began a voyage of danger, under the best of conditions; with the wind blowing as it was, it was a hazardous undertaking; but in the dark, it was doubly so. The banks were abrupt, the wind from the west, and by keeping in touch of the shore with our paddles, we slowly coasted across the island, till the shapes of tall trees overhead told us we were near the shanty.

How often since that, I have wondered how we ever made that

trip and found the hut; but we did it. We built a fire in the hut, and by its light we found, carefully laid up, a loaf of dry bread some woodchopper had left, and having killed a duck, we roasted it over the fire and feasted on roast duck and bread, and chatted and talked till sleepy, then stretched ourselves on the wooden bunks in the shanty and went to sleep. It must not be thought there was much comfort in the woodman's shanty, but it was a shelter from the fierce west wind. There were no blankets, nor even straw in the bunks. We were glad to be even sheltered from the cold wind, however. It was a long, weary night, but daylight came at last.

As soon as it was light enough to see to shoot, Sam went out to see the river and if possible get a buck or two, while I roasted what remained of yesterday's catch, which was scant enough for two hungry hunters. Sam returned and reported the main river too rough yet to venture on with our light canoe. Here we were, two men on an island, one of many miles long, with [the] main river on the east, and several wide waterways or sloughs on the west between us and the mainland. Thus we were obliged to wait till the wind ceased blowing, ere we could leave the island.

After breakfast, we both went to

the bank on the main river, to wait for the going down of the wind. It was cold; neither one had overcoat or gloves, and we were forced to keep moving to keep warm. Noon came, and still the gale swept the waves aloft. Toward evening, to add to our misery, there came a fierce shower of rain and sleet, and wet us through. After the rain, the wind increased in force. We feared to leave the river, being anxious, if the wind ceased blowing as the sun went down, to hasten across the cold water. We gathered a huge pile of driftwood and succeeded, after many trials, in lighting a fire. Everything was wet and it was very difficult to get the wet wood to burn. The sun went down, angry and red. We watched the wind-tossed waves from beside the huge fire we had built. The ground was too wet and cold to lie down on,

and weariness began to overcome us, to say nothing of hunger, which had become intense by this time, for we had been unsuccessful in killing any more game. However, we gathered brush and piled it near the fire, and lay down on that to catch, if possible, a little sleep. But the cold was so severe, we had to keep turning to keep warm; one side freezing, the other roasting.

The long, wretched night passed at last, and day came; but no cessation of the wind. Storm bound and miserable, wet, cold, and hungry, stiff and sore, we roused ourselves and sought for something to eat. One poor little duck was all we could find that day, and that seemed only to aggravate our hunger. It did seem strange, but the very ducks were hid away, or refused to venture to face the storm. We wandered up

and down the bleak river shore, and at last resolved to seek the old shanty and spend another night within its walls; but on further thought, we resolved to risk a move, one in the canoe, and one on shore, and coast along down the river. On reaching the sloughs, or waterways, we both entered the canoe and crossed them. Several times the water splashed into the little boat, and as many times we were in danger of sinking. We could not have lived twenty minutes in the cold water, if we had been plunged into it, even if we could have kept on the surface so long, but by great care and skill, keeping close under the bank as much as possible, we finally reached the mainland and thus the town, some four miles below where we were held upon the island. It was evening, just before dark, when we carne ashore there, and recognized the boat of a friend who was looking for us. We soon found him, and I got into his boat while Sam paddled the canoe, keeping close to the larger boat; thus we crossed the wide river. It was late at night when I carefully let myself into my own home, and found my way to my wife's room. I found her wide awake, a bright light in her room, and as I opened the door and walked in, she turned pale and for a moment was silent, then she said, "You're a pretty fellow, aren't you? Where have you

been?" A little shamefacedly, I answered, "Aren't you glad to see me? I'm hungry! Can you give me something to eat?"

And the baby looked up from the bed and laughed, "Papa, papa!"

—"Biography of Patriarch
Alexander Hale Smith,"
(January 1911) 15-19.

Baptism

ALEX HAD SHOWN but little interest in religion until his brother Joseph and mother Emma affiliated with the RLDS Church in 1860.

—"Biography of Patriarch
Alexander Hale Smith,"
(January 1911) 16.

During this period, Alexander experienced an encounter with the Holy Spirit. Alex wrote:

My Brother, David, joined the Church two years before I did. When my brother, David, was baptized I refused to go down to the water and see him baptized. I stood on the hillside afar and watched his baptism. God was working with me.

. . . I was taken sick. My mother was our doctor previous to this, and when she came to me and said, "Alexander, I can do no more for you," I felt as though I was lost.

My wife came to me, and said, "Shall I send for the elders?" My wife was not a member of the Church, neither was I. I was astonished. I said to her, "Have you any faith?"

"If I had not some faith I would not have asked you to let me send," she answered. " [I said:] You may send."

She sent for my brother, Joseph. He came into the room. He put his hands upon my head. "Why," he says, "boy, you are very sick." "Yes, I know I am sick." "What can we do for you?" "I don't know." "Do you believe that God can heal you?" I answered, "Joseph, I don't believe; I know that God can heal me, if He will. It is not the question as to whether He can, because I know He can if He will."

. . . He walked away from me, and as he walked away he said, "I know, we can't help you." My heart sank. I did not realize that I had had any faith that He might help me until that moment. He turned around, looked at me, and said, "Shall we administer to you?" I answered, "Yes."

He came and laid his hands upon my head, anointed me with oil. I was in that state of mind that I watched what that man said. I watched his prayer. I wanted to be satisfied that it was of God, that it was not the power of man nor of the adversary. And when he had finished praying, I said in my heart, "No power but the power of God will answer that prayer." In fifteen minutes I fell asleep, broke out in profuse perspiration; slept all day and all night.

The next morning I got up and put on my clothes, and was ready to go to work. But I was weak. I met my brother, David, and the first question he asked was, "Are you now ready to be baptized?" I said, "No."

The second day I met him. He asked, "Are you ready to be baptized?" "No." The third time I met him and he asked the same question, I said, "Yes, let us go and see Joseph." He [Joseph] went and baptized me.

—Alexander H. Smith, "My Heritage," Sermon, Kaukura, Tahiti, November 10, 1901, *Vision* No. 53 (July 2006) 21–22.

Alex's baptism was reported by John Shippy in the *Herald*: Joseph III "has baptized two lately, and his Bro. Alexander was one of them."

—John Shippy, "Good News from Iowa," *Herald* 3, no. 2 (August 1862): 43.

Alex's wife Elizabeth also requested baptism that same year. Alex and Elizabeth attended the "Olive Leaf Branch" of the Reorganization which met in the Red Brick Store at Nauvoo.

—"Biography of Patriarch Alexander Hale Smith," (January 1911) 14.

Ordination

ALEX DESCRIBED the next phase of his calling:

My call to the ministry was after this wise: The branch to which we belonged, called the "Olive Leaf," was in need of a teacher; and at a meeting for the purpose of electing officers, a member arose and nomi-

Engraving of Red Brick Store, in the 1880s.

nated my name and moved that I be ordained, and then bore testimony that the Spirit witnessed to him that it was my calling. Imagine, if you can, my surprise. My feelings were such, I scarce realized that what he said was in earnest, until my elder brother arose and confirmed the testimony and supported the motion. When I fully realized what was being done, I sprang to my feet and objected. I held a very exalted idea of what a teacher in the Church of Jesus Christ ought to be, and I knew I did not fill the measure of requirements a teacher should possess. I was young, inexperienced, ignorant of the law of God and the order of his church, had been a wild, thoughtless boy; and in no sense, in my own estimation, was I worthy to be made a teacher over members who had been in the church nearly as many years as I had been in the world. The task seemed altogether too huge an undertaking for me, and I tried to avoid it, for I felt that the office of teacher was one of great importance in the church. I argued that I could not talk in meeting—it was out of the question; but I was met with the objection that my plea was not well made, as I had already been speaking twenty minutes very rapidly. Not wishing to appear rebellious, I finally consented to do the best I could, and was ordained

a teacher.

—Alexander H. Smith, "Early Ministerial Experiences," *Autumn Leaves*, 10, no. 12 (December 1897): 529.

THE DUTIES OF a teacher, are described in the Doctrine and Covenants, CofC Section 17:11; LDS 20:53-59:

Doctrine & Covenants

11 The teacher's duty is to watch over the church always, and be with, and strengthen them, and see that there is no iniquity in the church, neither hardness with each other; neither lying, backbiting, nor evil speaking; and see that the church meet together often, and also see that all the members do their duty-and he is to take the lead of meetings in the absence of the elder or priest and is to be assisted always in all his duties in the church, by the deacons, if occasion requires; but neither teacher nor deacons have authority to baptize, administer the sacrament, or lay on hands; they are however to warn, expound, exhort, and teach, and invite all to come unto Christ.

Church Appointment

William Wallace Blair, 1863.

ALEXANDER'S FIRST mission appointment on behalf of the church was to Council Bluffs, Nebraska, with W. W. Blair in 1863.

—"Biography of Patriarch Alexander Hale Smith," (January 1911) 144.

W. W. Blair recalled:

Brother A. H. Smith was appointed to travel and preach with me the ensuing fall and winter.

—Frederick B. Blair, comp., *The Memoirs of President W. W. Blair* (Lamoni, Iowa: Herald Publishing House, 1908), 92.

Alexander recalled, "In the spring of 1864 I was called and ordained an elder; and from the very first effort, as an elder, my experiences have been of an interesting character."

Alex was immediately given charge of the St. Louis District. His ministerial burden became discouraging at times. Writing to Charles Derry, Alex explained:

I can not get the Elders in my district to work with the energy I would like. If they would only fill appointments and keep open places that I get open, it would be all I would ask of them.

—Alexander H. Smith, Letter, February 4, 1866, P19, f33, CofC Archives.

These experiences helped Alex better understand his ministerial aspirations, which he expressed in his 1864 journal:

"May God enable me to live in such a manner that I may be as firm as my Father and Uncles were in proclaiming the gospel."

—Alexander H. Smith, Journal, 1863-64, P2, J91, January 11, 1864, page 100.

Charles Derry's Visit

Charles Derry.

Alexander H. Smith, ca. 1863.

ALEX RETURNED HOME by December **1863.** A new convert to the RLDS Church, Charles Derry, visited Nauvoo about that time and described Alex:

Alexander Smith is not so tall as David, nor so heavy as Joseph. Is of light complexion, free and sociable, intelligent, and takes a great interest in the work. . . . All of the [the Smith boys] are workingmen. . . I never saw a family pay more respect to their mother than all three do.

—"Biography of Patriarch Alexander Hale Smith," (January 1911) 146.

Alex, David, and Joseph III.

Civil War

ALEX CUT SHORT his church responsibilities and joined the Union Army in 1864. After a brief enrolment, Alex was discharged in November of that year.

Master *of the* Mansion

Mansion House and Hotel wing,
drawing by Jack Garnier.

MMA GAVE Alexander a deed to the Mansion House and grounds in 1864. During this period, even while supporting his family, Alexander performed missions in western Iowa and southern Illinois. Vida was born, January 1865, in old room Number 10 near the end of the hall in the hotel wing of the Nauvoo Mansion.

In May 1865, RLDS missionary W. W. Blair visited Emma and Alexander at Nauvoo.

May 9, 1865

I parted...to prosecute a mission to St. Louis, Missouri, as requested by the late conference. I proceeded on to ... Nauvoo, Illinois, the 15th. While there I had an interview with Sister Emma, the widow of Joseph the Seer, and her son Alexander. She stated that in the spring of 1844 a council, composed of a number of the leading authorities of the church, was held in Nauvoo, and at its close Elder G. J. Adams came and said to her, rejoicing greatly, that one matter was now settled; they now knew who Joseph's successor would be,— it was little Joseph, for he had just seen him set apart under the hands of his father and others.

Brother Alexander H. Smith then related that Elder James Whitehead, a onetime secretary of Joseph the Seer, said to him not long before, that in the spring of 1844, just prior to the death of the Seer, "young Joseph" was set apart in a council by his father and others to be his successor, and that Bishop Whitney, Doctor Bernhisel, W. W. Phelps, Alpheus Cutler, Willard Richards, and, he thought, John Taylor were present on that occasion; also that Bishop Whitney held the horn of oil; and further, that Joseph the Seer afterward stated to the Saints from the public stand that he was no longer their prophet, and, putting his hand on young Joseph's head, he said, "This is your prophet. I am going to rest."

—*Memoirs of W. W. Blair,*
116-17.

Olive Branch Presiding Elder

Joseph Smith III, ca. 1865.

JOSEPH III MOVED TO Plano, Illinois, in January 1866. The Olive Branch at Nauvoo selected Alex to fill Joseph III's place as presiding elder. Alex described the impact of the loss of Joseph III in a letter to Charles Derry.

Joseph [III] is now in Plano. So the main attraction of this place has been removed. Perhaps the Saints will realise the inestimable value of the teaching they were wont to hear while he stayed here. Oh Bro Charles I sometime, think if preaching and a good example were needful to fit the Saints for Sion or Zion the Saints of this place have had both & if they heed them not where will rest the condemnation. I feel that if there never was another word of exhortation to come to this people here, there has been enough said already to damn them past redem[p]tion (almost) if they heed not what has been said in their hearing.

My mission calls me into the field constantly but the cares of my family will not let me spend all my time in the service of my Master. My desire is to be set-at-liberty and freed from the encumbrance which bind me away from my calling.

Not that I would like to free my self from my family no no not that. But I would like to be satisfied that their wants were sup[p]lied so they would not suffer then I would spend all my time in the work of the Lord. I am doing my best as it is and by the blessing of God I've been able to get along, and labor some in my calling. I now have appointments for some three weeks ahead & to-morrow I go six & 1/2 miles east of here to preach a funeral Sermon at 11 o'cl[ock] Bro Revel goes with me & I pray that the Spirit of God may be with me also for if I have it not I shall most miserably fail. Oh the harvest is more than ready & the reapers are so few that it seems that the work will not be accomplished in the time allotted. When I meditate on this subject it seems to me that I am all unworthy to be called a servant of God. What can I do to forward the work. The work is so great and the instruments so weak. If they many of them are as weak as I am they have need indeed of the help of Gods spirit to assist them and lead them into all truth to stay their feeble Knees when they tremble and faint by the wayside and to unloose their stammering tongues when they stand as witnesses for the cause of Christ. You who have felt the assistance of the spirit know how much I need that same help so I ask you to pray God that I may be firm in my faith & have the spirit of God to help me in my ministry.

—Alexander H. Smith, Letter to Charles Derry, Nauvoo, Illinois, January 10, 1866, P19, f33, CofC Archives.

Plano, Illinois.

Pacific Slope Misson

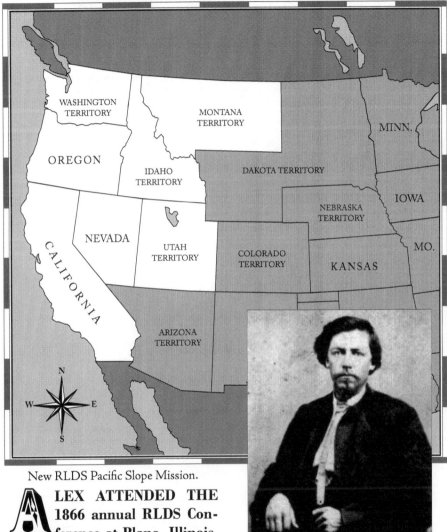

New RLDS Pacific Slope Mission.

Alexander, ca. 1866. Courtesy Buddy Youngreen.

ALEX ATTENDED THE 1866 annual RLDS Conference at Plano, Illinois. During the conference, Alexander was placed in charge of a newly created RLDS Pacific Slope Mission. Following ordination as a high priest, he began to prepare for his cross-continent journey.

—"Biography of Patriarch Alexander Hale Smith," (April 1911) 148.

Joseph Smith III, ca. 1866.

Alex gave Elizabeth a fifty cent piece. Photograph of Elizabeth Kendall Smith, courtesy of Buddy Youngreen.

In preparation for his absence, Alex stockpiled provisions for Elizabeth and little Fred A. In addition, local RLDS members promised to provide assistance as needed. On May 20, 1866, Alexander placed all the money he had, fifty cents, in Elizabeth's hand and told her good-bye. With his missionary companion, William Anderson, Alexander set out overland for California. James A. Gillen, whose mission objective was Utah, also travelled with them.

The RLDS missionaries ventured on their own to Fort Kearny then joined a LDS emigrant train of 250. Alexander gave his name as Alex Hale and attempted to keep their identity a secret. He wrote:

The train was a large one and consequently moved slowly, travelling only from fifteen to thirty miles a day. We soon discovered what we were watched very closely, and speculation was rife as to who we were. Several efforts were made to draw us out, to reveal our object in

RLDS 1866 Western Mission

Missionary traveling companions: William Anderson, Alexander H. Smith, and James A. Gillen.

crossing the plains; but for a time we remained unknown to them. At our first meal after joining the train, we were watched, and when we asked a blessing upon our food it was immediately reported to the captain that we were either apostate Mormons or Josephites, as no other class of religionists continued to keep up service and have prayer and ask a blessing upon the food so long after striking the plains. . . .

About the third day out from Laramie one of their number came to me and said he was in charge of the corral guard and was making

Fort Laramie, sketch by by J. Rulon Hales, "Mormon Trail," American Pioneer Trails Association (Manchester, NY: Clarke Press, 1947).

Mormon emigrant wagon train, sketch by by J. Rulon Hales, "Mormon Trail," American
Pioneer Trails Association (Manchester, NY: Clarke Press, 1947).

a list of all the names of the able-bodied men in order to organize more perfectly for the protection of the train. I at once recognized that it was simply a subterfuge to learn who we were. I told him at any time he wanted one of us men to let me know and I would furnish the man. This did not satisfy Captain Ricks, so I gave them our names, except that I only gave him my first and second name; so my name on his list was Alex Hale. My purpose in doing this was to avoid any undue curiosity among the emigrants, for if it was known there was a son of the martyred Prophet in the train,

there might be too many questions, and confusion ensue, or a collision on religious matters, which we desired to avoid while on the plains.

—"Biography of Patriarch
Alexander Hale Smith,"
(July 1911) 269-70.

Alex Hears Singing

Recreated photo of Alex scouting.

ONE DAY, while scouting in advance of the train, Alexander climbed an isolated hill. As the train passed by, Alexander heard singing. When he realized that the song was "We Thank Thee, O God, for a Prophet," Alexander knew they had figured out he was a son of Joseph Smith. Alex reminisced:

About this time a little incident occurred which pleased me, and left a pleasant memory to relieve some of the strain which affected us. One day I was assigned the position of advance guard. I mounted our pony, and rode out in advance of the train. We were in the mountains and traveling among them, small and

great. As I rode along I noticed a beautiful little mountain to the right of the train as we advanced—that kind of a hill called sugar loaf, because of its shape. The idea at once occurred to me that I could obtain a fine view of our route from its top, so I climbed up its sides, which by the way were quite steep towards the top, and when I reached it I was more than repaid for my labor. Of course I had to dismount and lead "Billy," as he could hardly scramble up with my assistance. I wish I could describe the scenery as viewed by me upon this mountain among mountains, detached and alone it stood, like a sentinel doing duty there among his fellows, grand, noble, and inspiring. As I stood resting my elbow on the neck of my horse, taking in the beauty of the scene, there came upon me a feeling of awe and reverence for the nobility and magnitude of the works of God; and while this feeling was upon me I became conscious of sweet musical vibrations of sound filling the air all around me. The volume of sound seemed at first above me, and I unconsciously looked upward to solve the mystery. Gradually the music seemed to draw near and tune and words came out full and distinct in singing. It was human voices, but I am sure angelic singing could not have affected me more just then. It was the emigrants as they passed around the base of the mountain. Whether they saw me and had been informed who I was, I had no way of knowing; but the words of the hymn led me to think so. These were a band of good singers and they were singing, "We thank thee, O God, for a prophet." I have heard the hymn sung by a good many choirs, including the famous Salt Lake City choir, since then; but never have I heard it equalled, as it was sung at the base of my little mountain.

—"Biography of Patriarch
Alexander Hale Smith,"
(July 1911) 270-71.

Prophet. (S. H. 58)

PUBLIC WORSHIP.

70. P. M.

WE thank thee, O God, for a Prophet
    To guide us in these latter days;
We thank thee for sending the Gospel
    To lighten our minds with its rays;
We thank thee for every blessing
    Bestowed by thy bounteous hand;
We feel it a pleasure to serve thee,
    And love to obey thy commands.

2 When dark clouds of trouble hang o'er us,
    And threaten our peace to destroy,
There is Hope smiling brightly before us,
    And we know that deliv'rance is nigh;
We doubt not the Lord nor his goodness,
    We've proved him in days that are past;
The wicked who fight against Zion
    Will surely be smitten at last.

3 We'll sing of his goodness and mercy;
    We'll praise him by day and by night;
Rejoice in his glorious Gospel,
    And bask in its life-giving light:
Thus on to eternal perfection
    The honest and faithful will go;
While they who reject this glad message,
    Shall never such happiness know.

This hymn was included in the 1870
RLDS hymnal.

Devil's Gate

FARTHER ALONG THE route, Alex's party reached Devil's Gate. Alex recalled:

Miles [of] travel by the road brought us to the Sweetwater River, at the gap in the mountains where the river rushes through, called the Devil's gate. Sometime in the dim past the mountains by some throe of nature have been cracked or broken, as a huge cut, clean from top to base, and moved apart; and the river taking advantage, rushed through and has ever since kept its channel, although huge quantities of rock have from time to time fallen from the ragged walls on either side,

which rise thousands of feet, sometimes perpendicularly, sometimes overhanging, and sometimes receding, raising upward, making a grand sight, which to be appreciated must be seen. It was thought that parties could pass through the gate on foot, but teams and horses must go around the point of the mountain by the road. It was Bro. J. A. Gillen's turn to drive our team, so William and I started out on foot. As we reached the outlet where the cold, clean water came tumbling over the rocky way, seeming glad to escape and rush away towards the plains, I determined to climb to the top, and cross the mountain, rather than risk a long, weary tramp back in case we

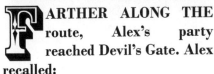

could not get through. I suspected that we would have to cross the rapid running stream several times ere we emerged from the canyon or the other side. I knew the water was very cold, and that to cross meant to plunge in and wade it, so I concluded to scale the mountain. I found the ascent was rough, but not of a hazardous nature, and as I climbed upward I found an abundance of interesting matter, which well repaid me for my labor. But ah! when I reached the summit what a grand sight was spread out before me! And as I turned and looked back the way we had come, I could see the wagon trail winding around the huge rock in the desert; and away towards the east the vast plain which seemed limitless; and to the south I could see occasionally the glint of silver as the river came in sight in its meanderings; while to the west lay a valley, a beautiful valley; and beyond, range upon range of rugged mountain scenery. North of me was the deep chasm, with the mountain rising higher and thus cutting off any extended view in that direction I sought out a fine resting place beneath a rugged pine tree, and rested and enjoyed myself until the sun's rays warned me that I better begin my descent. . . . I noticed a gummy substance exuding from the bark of a sugar pine, or balsam fir tree; I

gathered some, intending to try it on my sore hand. I started to descend, and the way seemed easy for a time, and I made my way down what seemed to be a hollow or depression. The soil was light and dry, and my feet would sink into it, leaving a well-defined trail. As I passed along I noticed tracks leading downward, but I soon came to the end of the depression, and as the track led on I approached what at first seemed a bench or abrupt drop off. I carefully crept to the edge and looked over. I fully expected to see the rocks but a few feet below, for the tracks plainly led right over the edge; but imagine my dismay as I looked over, away down, down, five hundred feet or more I saw the waters of the river rushing madly through the rocky channel, roaring like a torrent! I was not long creeping away back up from that route and onto more secure ground, for I imagined that light, loose soil was creeping, creeping down over that fearful verge to the depths below. I finally made my way down on the western slope of the mountain, where I could distinctly hear the people conversing, and where they had gone into camp. I climbed out on a huge pile of rocks where I could see every movement in the valley. Professors Savage and Ottinger were in the train, photographers, taking views, and I saw them getting ready to take a view of the very mountain side I was climbing down. I could plainly hear all they said, but I shouted as loud as I could and for a long time, it seemed to me, but they could not see me. I waved my hat and shouted; but it was no use; I could not get them to see me. It seemed to me that I could pitch a stone right in among them. I continued my downward course until I finally reached the camp and looked up. I saw the point I stood upon when I made such frantic efforts to attract their attention, and lo, it was fully one half mile away. William had made his way up through the gate by wading some places waist deep in the cold water.

—"Biography of Patriarch
Alexander Hale Smith,"
(July 1911) 272-74.

Later, nearer their objective, Alex visited Cache Cave:

We reached Cache Cave at the head of Echo Canyon, quite a large cave near the summit of the mountain, to the right of the wagon trail. We visited the cave and found the walls and the ceiling covered with names carved in the sandstone. I wanted to have my name registered on the tablets of this natural album. I sought in vain for space on the walls, but by standing up in my saddle on the back of my pony I found space right in the very top of the cave. I carved my name standing up on my horse to do it.

—"Biography of Patriarch
Alexander Hale Smith,"
(July 1911) 276.

SAVAGE & OTTINGER
GREAT SALT LAKE CITY
UTAH

Into *the* Basin

John Smith, Alex's cousin, met the wagon train as it entered the Valley.

WHILE DESCENDING the rim of Salt Lake Basin, the company was met by LDS Patriarch John Smith, Alexander's cousin.

At last we reached the rim of the basin, crossing Little Mountain, we turned down through Parley's Park, on the headwaters of Cottonwood, and on down through Cottonwood canyon. In this canyon we met some horsemen. Among them was my cousin, John Smith, patriarch of the Utah Church, oldest son of Hyrum Smith the Martyr. I . . . was greeted quite warmly by cousin John and those with him. . . . John turned . . . with me, and we rode together into the Great Salt Lake Basin, my cousin pointing out to me the points of interest as we entered the valley.

—"Biography of Patriarch Alexander Hale Smith," (October 1911)394-95.

When the RLDS missionaries reached Salt Lake City, cousin John invited them to stay in his home.

Emma Denounced

Emma Smith Bidamon.

President Brigham Young. Courtesy of the LDS Church History Library.

DURING ALEXANDER'S visit to Salt Lake City, Brigham Young publicly denounced Alexander's mother, saying:

—Brigham Young, Address, October 7, 1866, Brigham Young Papers, LDS Church History Library.

Emma . . . has made her children inherit lies. To my certain knowledge Emma Smith is one of the damnest liars I know of on this earth; yet there is no good thing I would refuse to do for her, if she would be a righteous woman.

Cousinly Correspondence

From California, Alexander corresponded with his cousin Samuel H. B. Smith in Utah.

CONTINUING ON TO California, Alexander and William Anderson visited a small branch of the Reorganization at Jack Valley, Nevada. There they sold their team and wagon and travelled to Sacramento, California, by stage.

While in Utah, Alexander felt that, on matters of their religious differences, members of his family were being less than frank with him. Alex perceived that they were unwilling or unable to share openly. Upon reaching California, Alexander attempted to determine whether his cousins, Samuel Harrison Bailey Smith and John Smith, were constrained in some way, or simply did not wish to discuss religion.

San Francisco Nov 19 <1866>
Cousin Samuel

I seat myself to write you a few lines to inform you of my health and safety.

I have no reason to complain except that my pants are getting to[o] small around the waiste [sic]. I have gained 20 lbs since I came into California. I find the climate agrees with me.

I desire to know of you if you are at liberty to write your true sentiments to me upon the work of God in these last days.

I do not wish you to feel hurt at my thus writing to you my desires.

I would be glad if we could meet each other on an equal footing, not fearing to speak our true principles to each other.

I feel that it is for the interest of the Smith Family to be united, Both Spiritualy [sic] and temporally.

You know I did not fear to speak my firm convictions while in your presence, and I do not fear the result of my so speaking, my only fear is that, Those most interested in your destruction will hedge you in and bind you by false covenants that you cannot make your escape when you would, For the time is not far hence when God will favor the chosen seed and punish all false sheperds [sic].

Oh Samuel break off your allegiance to that false power while you are young and yield yourself a servant[t] of God breaking down error and establishing truth on the sure foundation of the Law of God.

Be not entangled in the many secret organisatons [sic] of the valleys For God does not work in darkness.

That sprit of revenge that is taught there is contrary to the character of Christians or Saints of the most high God. But I'l[l] plead no more until I hear from you. I am as ever your loving Cousin

—Alexander H. Smith, Letter to Samuel H. B. Smith, San Francisco, November 19, 1866, MS 17756, f13, LDS Church History Library.

San Francisco Jan 19th [18]67
Cousin Samuel

Your note of the 8th Inst receive, this morning. Was glad to hear from you. Of your welfare and freedom to write your opinion or sentiments on the Word of God. Yet I deplore the feeling expressed in your wish not to enter or commence a war with the Smith family. I do not understand that a candid examination of the Laws of God (on which we both claim to be founded) would inaugurate a War between us. So far as my feeble efforts will accomplish a unity in the family. I mean to exert them to that end. There has been already too great an enmity existing between us. There seems to have been a fear of each other that is altogether uncalled for. There yet seems to be a mighty gulf between us, and whenever I have attempted to meet you and your division of the house to compare notes and arrive at an understanding I am shown that gulf and am told that any effort of mine to remove That [sic] obstacle will be the signal for the opening of a war between the Smith Family.

I truly did try to speak in plainness when I was there. I spoke a[s] God gave me utterance. And I had hoped that what I said to you & John would have more effect for good than for evil. My heart feels sad when I see the division of our house (That is speaking of the whole family). And I would do much to bring about a reunion, but as I have said before every attempt I make I find an unwillingness upon the part of those I wish to labor for, to assist in the work. As I said when [I] was with you so say I again I do not fear an investigation of these mighty differences. I rather seek investigation, nor do I feel that a correspondence upon these principles between you and I would commence war between the Smith Families. If I did I never would scratch a line to any of you. I speak for my self I allow no man nor set of men to speak for me. And it was this independent spirit that prompted me to ask you if you were at liberty to do the same, understanding as you know I do some of the order of your endowment covenants I feared you would not let the man be made manifest

Samuel you speak of exhibiting the character of my Father in my speaking in boldness, well I trust you will give me credit when I say those very firm convictions have taken such deep root and have so absorbed in a manner my existence That to compel me to yeald [sic] them would destroy my faith in God, and his laws that were given for our salvation, upon which the Church is founded. Samuel I could forgive very severe language from you or any of the rest of the family. In your letter you ask me to forgive you if any thing should esc<a>pe your pen to injure my feelings. I find nothing offensive in your letter to forgive. But I fear you cannot forgive me for my blunt plain blundering way of writing. But as God knows my heart I mean no harm nor offense to anyone much less to those I love. You express yourself that you would be much gratified if the Smith family could see matters in the same light. The word does not express the one half my feelings in case such an event should take place. Truly you said very little when I was there, yet I hoped I saw an under current to your feelings you did not express in words.

If this be so let me know that I may not build on a false foundation in my hope. You say you do not think you could say any thing to change my views. How do you think a change is to be brought about when all the rest even to Geo. A. smith Think just as you do, and none no not one has the manhood to even try to teach us different from that we believe. You say that time will prove which is right. Time is a slow coach when one is waiting anxiously the solution of so all important a problem as ones eternal salvation in the celestial kingdom of God.

Aunt Agnes[Don Carlos's widow] is in tolerable good health for her She is never very strong Ina is well so are Mr. Picket & the Boys, Agnes lives down to Los Angeles. I have not seen her nor heard direct of her lately. I am in good health and I may say have been blessed beyond my most sanguine hopes thus far. You speak of my return as if it was a matter of no doubt in your mind. While I look on my ever seeing that City again as extremely doubtful. Though for all that I am glad to hear of your comfortable situation. Forgive all offenses & bad writing your Cousin May God bless you Alexander H. Smith.

—Alexander H. Smith, Letter to Samuel H. B. Smith, San Francisco, California, January 19, 1867, MS 17756, f13, LDS Church History Library.

Agnes Smith Pickett, 1860s.

Alexander also attempted to maintain open communication with his cousin John Smith, writing in the same vein.

San Barnadino [sic] Feb. 8th 67
Dear Cousin

Your very kind letter has been received and duly considered. And as an ofset [sic] to your seeming neglect I plead guilty of the same fault in answering your letter.

I am thankful to you for your Photograph. And shall send you the means to pay for mine as soon as I can get money that I can send by Mail[.] I am glad to learn that you are as free as your letter seems to express. Yet your answer to my question is couched in such evasive terms that I am left in doubt as to your freedom. I know when you and I talked upon Matters that concern our eternal welfare you talked very evasively, and appeared under a constraint that prevented your expressing your real heartfelt convictions. You have told me to write freely and I am going to do so regardless of the seeming unwillingness of the part of some of my Cousins to come right out and express their true and firm convictions and give their reasons for their faith. You well know I justify a judiceious [sic] careful course yet I do not allow my manhood to entirely be taken from me by no <man> nor set of men nor yet combination of men. I am well aware that your position is such that you must needs act with great care, caution, and forethought, more particularly if you do not agree with those in more exalted positions in that organization[.] John I do not know how strongly you may be bound to those secrets, oaths, and combinations that have been established in that organisation to bind the members together, in the absence of the true love and power of God, which should bind the children of God more firmly together than any covenants or oaths that man can invent. I do not wish to begin a tirade of abuse against any person or persons but wish to careful[l]y investigate the Principles of the respective churches, and the individual right of the leaders of said churches, and I ask you to consider with me these points of importance to us. If you have the truth you need not fear an investigation, and if you have it I want it and if I have it I want you to have it. I do not wish you to think this a light matter and treat it as such But in the name of Isreals [sic] God I ask you to give heed to the dictates of the spirit of almighty God and seek your true position ere it be to late to retrieve what is lost of your time. And in this investigation I will try to show you plainly where in it is to your interest to come out of that modern Sodom.

Great events sometimes cast their shadow before and I feel impressed to warn you to get clear of the toils of those who wish you no spiritual good. If we will further continue this subject let me know untill [sic] then I am as ever your affectionate Coz

Alex H Smith

—Alexander Hale Smith, Letter to John Smith, San Bernardino, California, February 8, 1867, Joseph Smith Sr. Family Collection, VMSS 775, no. 2, box 2, folder 8, L. Tom Perry Special Collections, Harold B. Lee Library, Brigham Young University, Provo, Utah.

California Travels

THE

CHURCH, RECORD.

of the

EL MONTE, BRANCH,

of the.

CHURCH. OF. JESUS. CHRIST

of

LAT-TER-DAY, SAINTS.

TWELVE BRANCHES of the Reorganization were established in California by 1867. Alexander remained there for a year. Being away from his family for nearly eighteen months was a severe trial for him. Meanwhile, his daughter Ina Inez was born on November 1866.

Alexander returned home from California via Nicaragua, then by boat to New York. He landed in December 1867 and returned to Nauvoo. Alexander found that local Saints had not cared for his family as promised and that his wife and children were nearly starving.

—Alexander H. Smith, Biographical folder, CofC Library.

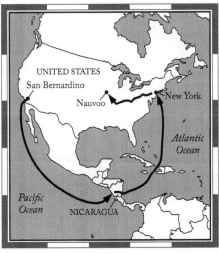

Alex's route home from California.

Correspondence *with* Joseph F. Smith

Joseph F. Smith.

ALEXANDER'S 1866 trip to Salt Lake City prompted a round of family correspondence. In a letter to Joseph III, Joseph F. apparently mentioned that Alex had kept in touch with his cousins John and Samuel but had failed to write to him.

From his home in Nauvoo, Alex penned a principled defense in response to Joseph F.'s comments:

Nauvoo, Illinois, Feb. 16th 1868

Cousin Joseph:

I have lately been permitted to read a letter from your pen directed to my Bro. Joseph in the which I am the principle object of converse, and so therein is a complaint against me for not writing to you with a charge that I write to both John and Samuel and thus show a preference. Let me say here I generally make it a rule to write to those who write to me. I have heard this same complaint before and was once persuaded to write—but received no response, consequently I concluded I was on forbidden ground and have remained silent in that direction since, and have thought if you desired a correspondence as you assert you would ere this have written to me. As far as I [k]now Joseph my feelings are as warm towards you as when we parted in your city. There were circumstances connected with my departure from Salt L. City which I deplored very much among which is the fact that you, John, and Samuel stood by and saw me and my things detained in a manner that you knew was unjust and not a voice from either of you was raised to prevent the injustice. Nay

Joseph I do not wish to dwell on these little exhibitions of love and friendship. Perhaps you can explain these little matters satisfactorily, Joseph there are other little testimonies that so far have led me to doubt the professions of friendship made by some men. Straws show which way the wind blows is a faithful and true saying. Although [I may see] the clear sky with light fleecy clouds bright with the rays of the sun denoting fair weather, a close scrutiny of the straws that support the grain in the field will bid me beware that the weather is treacherous.

The prompt act of Cousin Samuel on the night when we were talking before the theatre spoke volumes for his love and friendship. His placing himself between me and seeming danger of the which he seemed to fully realize denoted if he did not possess as strong a mind as some men, he did possess the manhood and love for his fellowman if nothing more to step between the object of his friendship and danger. But enough of this. I have done.

There is no one of our family who more thoroughly desires a reunion of the family than I do, and I am willing to do all in my power to bring it about. John and Samuel both acted. John in person came to meet me and went with me from place to place and also wrote to me in due time. These are some of the reasons why I wrote to them. But as there is a difference as you say in our faith, it need not make us enemies. Neither shall it upon my part. I as heartily despise catering to the views of others to curry favor as you possibly can, consequently my plain style of speech and writing. If I give offence I am ever willing when convinced of error to make amends. My family are well as I believe are the relatives.

Give my love to your wife and all the remaining relatives.

Alex H. Smith

—Alexander H. Smith, Nauvoo, Illinois, Letter to Joseph F. Smith, Salt Lake City, Utah, February 16, 1868, MS 18119, LDS Church Library.

Plano, Illinois

Plano, Illinois, RLDS Stone Church.

PLANO, ILLINOIS became the headquarters of the Reorganization in 1865. Alexander's family gathered to Plano in March 1868.

They first moved into three small rooms on the second floor of Joseph's house. That year, Alexander was reappointed to the Pacific Slope Mission, but was unable to leave right away. While preparing for his mission, he built a house for his family on a lot in the block adjoining the Plano Stone Church. Alex also helped construct the Stone Church. The building was dedicated November 15, 1868.

Another daughter, Emma Belle, was born in March 1869. In all, Alex and Elizabeth had nine children:

Frederick A., January 19, 1862
Vida Elizabeth, January 16, 1865
Ina Inez, November 27, 1866
Emma Belle, March 17 1869
Don Alvin, May 17, 1871
Eva Grace, March 1, 1874
Joseph George, May 7, 1877
Arthur M., February 8, 1880
Coral C. R., October 29, 1882

Don Alvin and Eva Grace Smith. Courtesy Gracia Jones.

Second Mission *to* California

RLDS Conference, David H. and Joseph Smith III standing in the front row to the left.

THE 1869 RLDS Conference reaffirmed Alex's reappointment to the Pacific Slope Mission and selected his brother David H. Smith to accompany him.

The recent completion of the transcontinental railroad enabled the pair to travel to their mission field by train.

Despite Alex's repeated visits to Utah, he was never seriously viewed as a potential successor to his father by western Mormons, but some believed David might one day fill that role.

—"Biography of Patriarch Alexander Hale Smith," (July 1912) 264.

Succession

David H. Smith.

Alexander H. Smith.

DAVID'S charismatic personality contrasted with Alexander's more natural reserve. David's "friendliness encompassed everyone, and he maintained no 'proper' distance from strong-minded Brighamites." Even Brigham Young once seemed to imply the possibility he would be succeeded by David Smith. During an 1866 address Brigham said, "When Joseph the Prophet was killed his wife Emma was pregnant. Joseph said previous to his death, 'She will have a son, and his name shall be called David, and unto him the Lord will look.' . . . . I am looking for the time when the Lord will speak to David, but let him pursue the course he is now pursuing, and he will never preside over the Church of Jesus Christ of Latter-day Saints in time nor eternity. . . . He has got to repent of his sins, and turn away from his iniquity, to cease to do evil, and learn to do well, embrace the Gospel of life and salvation, and be an obedient son of God, or he never can walk up to possess his right. It would be his right to preside over this church, if he would only walk in the path of duty. I hope and pray that he and the whole family will repent, and be a holy family."

—Valeen Tippetts Avery, *From Mission to Madness: Last Son of the Mormon Prophet* (Urbana: University of Illinois Press, 1998), 166-67; 168, quoting Brigham Young, "Brigham Young Addresses, 1865-1869," 5:116-19, Brigham Young Collection, LDS Church History Library.

Meeting *with* Brigham

Lion and Beehive houses. Brigham Young's office is the small building in the middle, ca. 1855. Courtesy of the LDS Church History Library.

ALEXANDER AND DAVID obtained an audience with Brigham Young, on July 17, 1869, accompanied by their cousins John, Samuel, George A. and John Henry Smith.

—"Biography of Patriarch Alexander Hale Smith," (July 1912) 259.

Anticipating this unavoidable encounter, Emma expressed anxiety to Joseph III by letter:

I hope they will be able to bear with patience all the abuse they will have to meet. I do not like to have my children's feelings abused, but I do like that Brigham shows to all, both Saint and sinner that there is not the least particle of friendship existing between him and myself.

—Emma Smith Bidamon, Nauvoo, Illinois, Letter, August 1, [1869], MS 9091, LDS Church History Library.

Alexander described the interchange:

We passed through two or three anterooms or connecting rooms between the Deseret News Office and President Young's private office, and were ushered into the presence of Brigham Young and about nineteen or twenty others; and the puzzle of our long wait was solved. Messengers had been sent out in the city to call in the principal men of the church to be present at the interview, and it took time to get them all in. There were Pres. Brigham Young, John Taylor, Daniel Wells, George A. Smith, Brigham Young, Jr., George Q. Cannon, J. P. Smith, John Henry Smith, John Smith, Samuel Smith, Joseph Young, Phineas Young, and a number of others whose names escape my memory now. From the imposing array of names, you can judge the interview was considered by President Young to be an important one. To say I was surprised does not fully express my feeling at this imposing array of the heads of the church there. I had simply called upon Mr. Young to request the use of the tabernacle, not expecting to meet so strong an array of talent.

We were formally introduced to all in the room, and after this ceremony, I simply announced the object of my call, telling President Young I understood that others were granted the use of the tabernacle when not in service by themselves, and as my brother David and I were there to represent the Reorganized Church we would like to be accorded the privilege to address the people from the pulpit of the tabernacle. Here let me explain a little. Three years before I had spoken in Line and Fox's Garden, a place of public resort in the city, and in my service I was opposed by my cousin, Joseph F. Smith, and in my answer to him I made use of some statements which displeased President Brigham Young; and ere my request was noticed I was called upon by him to take back or retract my statements. I told him I could not do so because they were strictly true, and I stood ready to prove them. He asked me where I got my information, and I remarked I had lived through the experiences of many of the events referred to, and did not need to have anyone inform me. He then asked me if my mother did not give me information. By this time so much had been said we were both getting warm and earnest in our converse. I answered, Yes sir, and I had more confidence in her statement than I did in his. This made him quite angry, and he began to abuse my mother, calling her "the damnedest liar that ever lived;" accused her of trying to poison my father twice, and also accused her of stealing my father's and Uncle Hyrum's picture, and his family ring, and withholding them from the church and the family, and other things of like nature.

I finally told him to stop; that what he had said was false and he knew it to be false. Of course this angered him still more.

Some one said, "We love you boys for your father's sake." I said that made no impression upon me, I expected to live long enough to make for myself a name, and have the people of God love me for my own sake.

At this President Young arose to his feet, clenched his fists, and shook them down by his side, raised upon his toes and came down on his heels repeatedly as he said, "A name, a name, a name. You have not got God enough about you to make a name. You are nothing at all like your father. He was open and frank and outspoken, but you; there is something covered up, something hidden, calculated to deceive."

I told him time would tell.

He then told me that article on marriage in the Book of Covenants had been written by Oliver Cowdery and published in the book directly in opposition to father's wishes.

I remarked, "President Young, unfortunately for your statement, that article with every other one in the book, used by the church previous to father's death, was laid before a general assembly of the church in solemn assembly, and indorsed by the whole church." I then chal-

Brigham Young, ca. 1869.

lenged him or any other authorized representative of the church there in Utah to meet us in discussion of the differences in faith and organization existing between us. I told him, "You say you have the truth, and that we are in error. If you have the truth, what need you fear? You are men in full vigor of mind and reason, we are but boys. If it is as you say you can easily overcome us, if we are in the wrong; but if it proves that we are right the sooner you get right the better. Unfortunately for us, a Mormon legislature has made laws prohibiting preaching upon the streets of the cities in Utah, so we are denied the means used by your missionaries in Europe to convert

Deseret Store and Printing Office, Salt Lake City, Utah, 1860s.

arose and said, "So far as I am concerned, I can soon express myself. After we whose hairs have grown gray in the service of God and after we have borne the heat and burden of the day in persecution and suffering, on land and sea, and have labored long and hard in heat and cold to build up the work and name for their father; for these boys to come now and ask us for the use of our houses to tear down what we have been so many years in building up, to me it is the height of impudence, and I will not give my consent to it." He was very much in earnest, his face was as white as death.

David then quietly arose to his full height and his face was also white but his words were calm, but oh, so full of sarcasm: "We will not deny that you have traveled far, suffered much, and labored hard to build up a name for our father, but what sort of a name is it? A name that we his sons are ashamed to meet in good society, and it shall be our life's work to remove from our father's name the stain you have heaped upon it."

None were so severe as George Q. Cannon. After an expression had been called for and given, President Young then turned to David and said, "No, David, we do not think it wise to let you have the tabernacle." As we arose and turned to go out, Mr. Young said, "Boys, don't let

thousands; but you have not made it a misdemeanor to preach upon the mountain side, and we propose to get the ears of this people, if we must needs preach on the mountain side."

President Young would no longer talk to me; so I said, "Come, David, let us go; it is useless to prolong this controversy." We arose to our feet, and David said, "Mr. Young, are we to understand that we are denied the use of the tabernacle?"

President Young then turned to his brethren, and said, "What do you say, brethren?" Several of them expressed themselves disapproving the letting us have it. The exact words of none come to me except those of George Q. Cannon. He this be your last visit; come again. I would gladly take you to my bosom if I did not think I would be taking a viper to my bosom that would sting me to death."

I told him he need not be alarmed, it was not likely after the reception we had just passed through, that we would visit either at his home or office. We went out, and the fight was on. . . .

It was quite a task upon my good nature to sit still and hear a man call my mother a liar, as Brigham Young did, and if I had not been in some sense prepared for it, I do not think I could or would have done so. Before leaving home on my mission, my mother called me in her room one day and had a long talk with me. Among other things she said: "Alexander you are going west on a mission to save souls. There are souls here right at home which are of just as much value to God as any of those to whom you are being sent, and so far as I am concerned of far greater value. You need not flatter yourself that you are going to win those old members of the church back to the paths of virtue and righteousness, for you will not be able to do so, at least none of those who were leaders here before they went west. They will none of them ever return, they have sinned away the day of grace, and I want to warn you and thus

put you on your guard. Don't you ever allow yourself to feel hurt or bad at anything they may say about me. They will say bad things about me. Don't let it worry you at all, for I had rather they would say evil things of me than good; they cannot hurt me, and it need not hurt you. I know them and I know the spirit they are of, at least the leaders of that people, and I tell you again you never will win any of them over to the church." I wondered at what my mother told me, and often pondered it in my heart, for I did have hopes that some day the Lord would soften the hearts of some of those men who knew the truth once and bring them back again to the primitive faith of the church.

Well, when Brigham Young was abusing my mother so to my face, my first impulse was to strike him, and quick as a flash I seemed to hear the words, "You are representing the Lord Jesus Christ," and then followed the words of my mother, "Do not let anything they may say offend or hurt you, they can't hurt me and I would rather they would speak ill than good of me," and at once I had myself in control.

—Alexander H. Smith, "Early Ministerial Experiences: No. 16," *Autumn Leaves* 14, no. 8 (August 1901): 349-52.

Visit *to* Don Carlos Smith's Family

A ring like Don Carlos Smith's gold ring.

IN DECEMBER 1869, Alexander and David left Utah and continued on to California carrying a heavy gold ring with them. It was one of three rings earlier presented to their father and "uncles Hyrum and Don Carlos by an admirer in Nauvoo." In San Francisco, they located Don Carlos's widow, Agnes Coolbrith, and her daughter, Josephine Donna Smith. The latter had rebuilt her life in California, not as a Mormon, but as "Ina D. Coolbrith," librarian, author and poet. Here, they presented Ina with her "father's gold ring . . . [which] became a prized possession."

—Avery, *From Mission to Madness,* 119.

Ina Coolbrith.

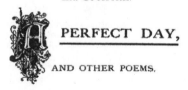

A PERFECT DAY,

AND OTHER POEMS,

BY

INA D. COOLBRITH.

AUTHOR'S SPECIAL SUBSCRIPTION EDITION.

SAN FRANCISCO:
1881.

The title page from a book of Ina's poems published in 1881.

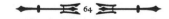

Plan *to* Enclose *the* Nauvoo House

The Nauvoo House as it might have appeared around 1870 before Lewis Bidamon removed some of the walls and enclosed the southwest corner of the building, retouched.

THOUGH FAR AWAY in the American West, Alexander was concerned for his mother's welfare. Lewis Bidamon had previously explored the possibility of enclosing a portion of the unfinished Nauvoo House as a means of providing better living arrangements for Emma. In the following letter, advocating for his mother's interests, Alexander urged this project along,

volunteering himself and his brothers to assist with the labor.

Salt Lake City Sept 12th 1869
My Own Dear Mother
This fine Sunday Morning I sit down to answer a kind good letter received from you. In your letter you seem anxious concerning us. I don't think there is the slightest need of fear. But still we shall use caution in our movements. We now contem-

plate remaining here until the latter part of November or the 1st of December. . . .

[If] Pa Bidamon does not still hold the idea of building the Navoo [sic] house as a residence, do you think he would make use of some of the material to build a cottage for you if he could get some assistance in the matter. Let me know Mother. I desire that you should not have so much house room to keep clean, nor so much running up and down stairs to do. Ask him about it.

I can not get it out of my head but that my greatest interest will always be at Nauvoo. So if he will use the means in his power to build a comfortable cottage home I will help him. But he must not try to build a castle, nor expect to build in the air, as we have to do with stubborn matter of the fact hard times and so must go slow at first. I can rely on the assistance of both David and Joseph in this matter. I shall expect some answers to this letter soon, as soon as you can conveniently confer with him and see what he will do.

Alexander H. Smith

—Alexander H. Smith, Letter to Emma Smith Bidamon, Salt Lake City, September 12, 1869. Transcription by Rick Grunder.

Lewis and Emma Smith Bidamon, retouched collage.

Return *to* Plano

The Alexander Smith house in Plano, Illinois, 1869.

IN EARLY SPRING 1870, news that Alexander's wife was seriously sick at Plano, Illinois, along with David's failing health compelled the Smith brothers to return east. Elizabeth had lung fever.

Emma Bidamon described the impact of this illness upon the extended family.

[Joseph's] oldest daughter was very sick with the lung fever, and she was so anxious to see me that her father sent for me when I got there Emma was better, her fever was checked but she was very weak, but I found my son Alexanders wife just taken with the same fever the day before I got there, and she grew worse for seven days before the fever abated. She was so very bad that Joseph telegraphed to Alexander who was then in Sanfrancisco [sic] Cal to come home, and he brought my son David home with him, who had been quite sick before they started for home, and I had to stay at Plano a week longer before Alex wife was well enough for me to leave her or David well enough to go home with me. . . .

—Emma Smith Bidamon, Letter to Mrs. (Emma) Pilgrim, March 27, 1870, Emma Smith Papers, P4, f43, CofC Archives.

Riverside Mansion

WITH ALEX'S continued urging, in the early 1870s Bidamon finally began to convert the Nauvoo House foundation into a cottage for Emma. He removed portions of the unfinished Nauvoo House construction and reused the bricks.

True to his promise, Alexander moved his family back to Nauvoo to help with much of the physical labor. Alex's daughter Vida recalled a serious incident when a section of the brick wall suddenly collapsed while being removed.

Father and others were trying to finish it. . . . Many of the workmen, my father with the rest, were seriously injured. . . . Father came walking up from the place of dust and confusion—Mother, white and wide-eyed on one side, and Aunt Julia on the other—with that awful wound in his head.

—"Biography of Patriarch Alexander Hale Smith," (April 1913) 220.

It could have been even worse, as moments before the collapse, Alex and Elizabeth's eight-year-old son, Frederick A., had been playing at the very spot where the wall fell.

Despite these setbacks, by their united labor, the residence was eventually enclosed, allowing Emma to spend her final years living in this finished portion of the Nauvoo House. Emma and Bidamon renamed the structure the Riverside Mansion. Emma continued supporting her family by caring for boarders.

Apostle

Alexander H. Smith, 1873.

Charles Wandell and Glaud Rodger.

ON APRIL 10, 1873, Alex was ordained an apostle and reappointed to Pacific Slope with James McKiernan. The missionary companions left for the west from Farmington, Iowa, on June 27, 1873.

—James McKiernan, Letter to Vida Smith, July 21, 1911, cited in "Biography of Patriarch Alexander Hale Smith" (July 1912) 275.

They stopped for a time in western Iowa. While there, Alexander received a letter from Joseph III urging him to hasten to the West to "attend to certain ordinations arranged by the April Conference. Father borrowed, on his own personal note, the money necessary for traveling expenses to the slope, Brother Calvin A. Beebe making the loan to him, and reluctantly and sadly he parted from Elder McKiernan."

Upon reaching California, Alexander set apart Charles W. Wandell and Glaud Rodger for a RLDS mission to Australia. The conference returned Alexander to California again in 1875.

—"Biography of Patriarch Alexander Hale Smith" (October 1912) 477.

Andover, Missouri, 1876-80

Alexander H. Smith family home at Andover, Missouri. Courtesy Gracia Jones.

ompleting a decade of missionary responsibility for California in 1876, Alex, who was then thirty-eight years old, needed a change. A spirit of gathering was emerging in the RLDS church. Members began to gather at Decatur County, Iowa, along the Iowa—Missouri border. Alex's birth in Missouri further heightened his own sense of urgency for the church's return to Jackson County. Alex scouted out the emerging colony and found a place "that appealed to his heart-call" nearby, "just over the line about a mile in Harrison County, Missouri." In order to take possession of his ideal farm, Alex entered into a substantial mortgage.

Alex returned to Nauvoo and began preparing his family for the move. His daughter Vida explained:

During the time of preparation for this move, Father found time to lift a voice in defense of the Master in old Hancock County. In April he met with his quorum in session at the semiannual Conference at Plano, Illinois, and soon after returning to Nauvoo from the Conference his goods were ferried over the Mississippi and loaded into a waiting car, among them being some stock and articles that were long-delayed payment for rent of the little farm. Among these, one fine, high-spirited gray colt called "Topsy"—a pet with all.

The bright, sunny April day was closing down. The children were trooping through the hall of the Nauvoo House to where Grandma stood spreading "pieces" for the hungry little band. The little mother sat wearily in the big rocker, tears of parting already shining in her eyes, although she thought the night lay between her and the last good-bye. The rooms at the Mansion looked sadly lonely, and as Grandmother stooped to tie a stray bonnet string or press into tiny hands a well-sugared biscuit, there was the tremor of sadness in the dear old hands, and the brown eyes overflowed. Soon they would all be gone, and how they would be missed.

Suddenly there came a shout from the front door, and some way in the hurry and bustle of the hour we were swept out of the loving arms of our grandmother, and from the brow of the hill I recall looking back to Grandmother standing with her hands shading her eyes from the western sunlight, a pathetic droop to the whole beloved figure. Father had discovered the [railroad] car was going that night and Mother had refused to go alone, so we were thus suddenly whisked away from the old home and Grandmother.

The setting sun gleamed in a thousand bright lights on the windows of the old homes, and touched the waters to a molten sea as we passed beyond the island, freshly green with springtime budding, and left the childhood home forever; and never again did my mother look upon the cherished friend of her life, her foster mother and ideal mother-in-law. All that she had been to my mother no pen can ever tell. That was the greatest sorrow of this change to a new home. It left the grandmother so lonely. For Father and Mother there were new scenes and unique experiences and making of new friends; for Grandmother the lonely days and sad memories in the old town.

—"Biography of Patriarch Alexander Hale Smith," (January 1913) 28-30.

Daughter Vida also described the setting of the new Smith home in Missouri:

In my mind's eye there is a picture of this country home, whose comfortable shelter we found a quarter of a mile back from the main road which runs east and west. A tangled bit of woodland lay between this road and the house, and a picturesque road wound downhill through it and up and down and up again, to the barnyard gate. There in the open glade facing the west stood the farmhouse, built of native timber and strongly built and sure. A drive through the barnyard and we entered the dooryard from the north, through a native grove of straight, smooth-barked bitternut trees, that grew almost to the kitchen door. The view to the south and west was one of wooded hills, with low, green bottomlands along the creek bed. . . . Looking from the house to the east, across the stretch of meadow, the eye rested upon a wide stretch of prairie, with the little hamlet of Andover near to the northeast, and still nearer, the schoolhouse and little graveyard. . . . It would be hard to find a spot differing as widely from the Nauvoo home, and yet it was beautiful, and certainly secluded and still.

—"Biography of Patriarch Alexander Hale Smith," (January 1913) 32-33.

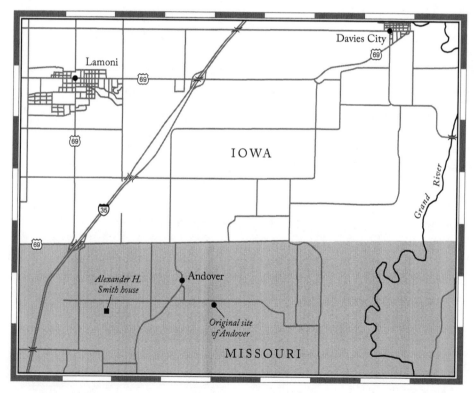

Alexander's home near Andover, Harrison County, Missouri, and Lamoni, Decatur County, Iowa. (Modern roads are indicated as a reference.) Cartography by John Hamer.

Alex's Qualities

Alexander H. Smith, ca. 1875.

PERHAPS Alexander's daughter, Vida, best described her father's courtly manner:

It was while living thus on the farm that we made the first really intimate acquaintance with Father, and formed the biggest estimate of his possibilities as a companion and a real chum. Those of us who were permitted to labor beside him, or take tramps into the woodland where he often spent whole long days cutting wood, or if granted to ride with him on some cherished expedition for pleasure or business, found him a delightful companion. As daughters we received from him, of course, deserved but gentle-voiced criticism of action or language, but coupled with it was always the same chivalrous, courteous, gentlemanly consideration that he expected other men to bestow upon us. To meet with his disapproval in conduct or speech was almost unerringly to be deserving of it. Long after I was a woman, and when far from his guiding hand, a woman of his acquaintance said to me, "I always thought your father's standard of womanhood very difficult to reach," and turning that sentiment over in the light of mature years, I have wondered if the standard of womanhood to all men is not measured by their conceptions of the goodness and virtue and strength of the women they knew best in childhood.

—"Biography of Patriarch Alexander Hale Smith," (April 1913) 219.

Emma's Death

DURING EMMA Bida-mon's final illness, her adopted daughter, Julia Middleton, called Alexander to their mother's bedside by telegram. When Alexander arrived, Emma was yet living. He wrote to his wife Elizabeth:

April 27, [1879] . . . Mother is gradually failing. . . Poor mother! Oh, Lizzie, it is hard to see her suffer so. . . . We are simply awaiting the end, and it seems to be near.

Alexander described Emma's last moments:

My mother raised right up, lifted her left hand as high as she could raise it, and called, Joseph. I put my left arm under her shoulders, took her hand in mine, saying, Mother, what is it, laid her hand on her bosom, and she was dead; she had passed away.

And when I talked of her calling, Sr. Revel, who was with us during our sickness, said, Don't you understand that? No, I replied, I do not. Well, a short time before she died she had a vision which she related to me. She said that your father came to her and said to her, Emma, come with me, It is

Emma Smith Bidamon, ca. 1875. Courtesy Liberty Hall, Lamoni, Iowa.

time for you to come with me. And as she related it she said, I put on my bonnet and my shawl and went with him; I did not think that it was anything unusual. I went with him into a mansion, a beautiful mansion, and he showed me through the different apartments of that beautiful mansion. And one room was the nursery. In that nursery was a babe in the cradle. She said, I knew my babe, my Don Carlos that was taken away from me. She sprang forward, caught the child up in her arms, and wept with joy over the child. When she recovered herself sufficient she turned to Joseph and said, Joseph, where are the rest of my children? He said to her, Emma, be patient, [a]nd you shall have all of your children. Then she saw standing by his side a personage of light, even the Lord Jesus Christ.

Alex advised his wife of Emma's passing:

April 30, [1879] ... The battle of life is over. Mother died this morning at 4 o'clock and 20 minutes.

Alex also faced demanding conditions upon his return home to northern Missouri. He described what he found to his friend William H. Kelley via letter:

On my return home after waiting and watching at mothers sick bed and death, I found my family much in need of my presence. Fred my oldest boy, was sick with chill fever and my work all at a standstill, so of course I had to doff my coat and go to work. I have not got the seed in the ground ... [but] purpose going into my mission this week, no preventing providence.

—Alexander H. Smith, Letter to W. H. Kelley, June 3, 1879, William Kelley Papers, P1, box 2, f5, item 35, CofC Archives.

Stewartsville, Missouri

Smith home at Stewartsville, Missouri.

BY 1881, ALEXANDER was finding it impossible to continue supporting his family by farming while serving in the mission field. Giving up this impossible struggle, Alexander and Elizabeth rented their Andover farm to Elizabeth's brother-in-law. Alex arranged a place for his family at Stewartsville, Missouri. Stewartsville was becoming a significant place of gathering for RLDS members in northwestern Missouri. Stewartsville also offered improved educational opportunities for the Smith children. Stewartsville saints promised to help Alexander construct a church mission house for his family.

—"Biography of Patriarch
Alexander Hale Smith,"
(July 1913) 294.

—"Biography of Patriarch
Alexander Hale Smith,"
(July 1913) 294.

**After the last wagonload of
furniture had been carted away
from the farm, Alex loaded his
family into the "home wagon."
Alex's daughter Vida, recalled,**

As we waited for Father's last
errand after some forgotten trifle,
Mother, casting a searching and sor-
rowful eye about the house yard,
spied the shining cover to her wash
boiler laying as it had dropped from
one of the wagons. She frugally
picked it up and tucked it into the
wagon at the side, then took her
place on her low spring seat, and
soon father joined us and the low
hung sun of a winter day glinted on
the windows of the farmhouse as we
looked back from Bethel church, a
mile to the west, before we passed
from the view of it.

—"Biography of Patriarch
Alexander Hale Smith,"
(April 1913) 230.

**The little town of Stew-
artsville "was a busy place. . . .
Besides its excellent public school,
it had a small college that was
well attended during the winter
months."**

**For the winter, Alex moved
into a church brother's one-room
house. Some members of the
family found temporary lodging
with others. In the spring, Alex**

joined with the Stewartsville and
German Stewartsville brethren in
building a mission house on a lot
situated on the northern edge of
town. Quick as the frame house was
enclosed, the scattered members of
our household and all household
goods were moved into this new
home [the family living in it during
the process of lathing and plaster-
ing] . . . . Mother took some comfort
in the new carpet and a few pieces of
new house furnishing that the sale
of some of the farm animals secured;
and with the money realized from
the sale of our old pet, the beautiful
gray Topsy horse, we secured a last-
ing monument to [its] memory in
a modest but sweet-toned Western
Cottage Organ, which came to be
known in the family as the "wooden
brother."

—"Biography of Patriarch
Alexander Hale Smith,"
(July 1913) 294-95.

While Alex "labored in the missionary field," the family spent the winters of 1881 and 1882 at Stewartsville, Missouri.

—"Biography of Patriarch Alexander Hale Smith," (July 1913) 295.

Independence, Missouri

Alexander Smith's home in Independence, Missouri, 1882–87.

FINALLY IN MARCH 1882, Alex gathered his family "to the spot of his dreams" in Independence, Missouri, and they made their home at 112 South Spring Street.

—"Biography of Patriarch Alexander Hale Smith," (July 1913) 295.

Right: Independence, Missouri, court-house tower, ca. 1880s.

Conference Photograph

RLDS Apostles A. H. Smith, W. H. Kelley, John Lake, Zenos Gurley Jr., and T. W. Smith.

CHURCH ATTENDEES gathered at Independence, Missouri, for the 1882 RLDS Conference. During the event, several conference participants posed for group photographs at F. C. Warnkey's Portrait Studio. Also, William Kelley's family, of Kirtland, Ohio, stayed with the Alexander Smiths during the conference.

My folks are more contented now than heretofore, as they are getting more aquainted [sic]. Thank you for your good wishes in our behalf, as to kindness manifest to you it is nothing. We are only too glad to have those who we can trust in whom we have confidence and love, to come and make our home their home. I should regret very much if you did not feel at home in my house. My wife is very sensitive and has for a long time felt that our brethren gave us the go by, and sought for better quarters. Well I tell her its all right, if they are better cared for and more contented, but she thinks it's on her account. So Will it did me good to have you with other of our Brethren make your home with me during conference.

—Alexander H. Smith, Independence Missouri, Letter to William H. Kelley, July 1, 1882, William H. Kelley Papers, P1, box 4, f1, item 33, CofC Archives.

Book *of* Mormon Printer's Manuscript

Book of Mormon Printer's Manuscript, *Zion's Ensign* Publishing Office, Independence, Missouri, 1903.

IN JULY 1883, David Whitmer consented to allow an inspection of the Book of Mormon Printer's Manuscript at his home in Richmond, Missouri, for comparison purposes against published versions. Alexander and Joseph III were part of the RLDS Committee conducting this inspection.

Joseph Smith, oldest son of Joseph Smith, the Martyr, the man by whom the Book of Mormon was translated and given to the world . . . was there at the request and selection of father Whitmer, directed by the Spirit; associated with him, also. . . . Alexander H. Smith, third son of Joseph Smith . . . were present as duly appointed representatives of the Latter Day Saints. . . .

Two years since Major Lewis C. Bidamon, who married Emma Smith, in 1847, and is in possession of the Nauvoo House, took up the corner stone referred to, in repairing and remodeling the dwelling into which he made a part of the premises. He found that the contents of the stone had been imperfectly preserved, water having penetrated the cavity. The manuscripts were water soaked and spoiled, a small section only being decipherable, the rest was mostly reduced to pulp, and on those portions not so reduced, the writing was faded out and illegible. A copy of the Doctrine and Covenants was with the manuscript, and the whole mass when dry crumbled to pieces at a touch. He forwarded, such part as could be handled, to us at Lamoni, where after a little exposure and handling it became entirely worthless even as a relic. If this copy thus accounted for was one of the two which it is alleged were made at the beginning, either the original, or the copy, the one which Elder David Whitmer has is the only one in writing in existence; and must be the basis from which any errors, if any have been made must be corrected.

—"It is often said that history repeats itself...." *Herald* 31, no. 34 (August 23, 1884): 537-38.

The *Saints' Herald* reported,

"Bro. Alexander H. Smith read the Palmyra copy, and Bro. W. H. Kelley the Plano copy; carefully noting each and every change that was discovered in the printed copies." The RLDS Church subsequent published an edition of the Book of Mormon on the basis of the committee's findings.

—"Book of Mormon Committee Report," *Herald* 31, no. 34 (August 23, 1884): 545.

Armstrong, Kansas

Armstrong RLDS congregation, ca. 1890.

WHILE LIVING AT Independence, Missouri, forty-four-year-old Alexander provided ministry to surrounding congregations. Alexander wrote,

Last week while laboring in Armstrong, [Kansas], I went to work on the saints' meeting house being erected there ... I went upon the scaffold to aid in putting on the cornice. We got too ... [many big men] on one corner and the scaffold broke and I would have got a bad fall but I caught on the cornice .... [Yet] I sustained ... internal injuries ... [and] am now laid up.

—Alexander H. Smith, Letter to E. L. Kelley, July 21, 1883, P58-1, f1, CofC Archives.

Financial Matters

IN ADDITION TO HEALTH limitations, Alex was falling behind financially. Excerpts from a series of letters to Edmund L. Kelly, in the RLDS bishopric, reveal Alex's growing concern:

[I have but little] . . . to meet a possible demand of $267.75—aside from the note . . . I paid Mr. May the dry goods merchant $67.85, my apple man $6.25, my grocers bill is $133.65 yet unpaid. . . . If I can only get out of this scrape. . . . I never felt so much like a criminal in my life, as I did yesterday. I could not help my feelings. I did feel ashamed to go up town, for fear someone would ask for what I could not give, and that was justly theirs to ask. It will be a long time I am thinking before I allow myself to so entangle myself again.

—Alexander H. Smith, Letter to E. L. Kelley, April 20, 1883, P12, f2, CofC Archives.

Alexander observed in another letter:

My oldest is about discouraged. She has tried hard to get a situation but has failed, and as I am not able to get her the many little flum[m]eries so dear to the young girls life in dress and otherwise, she has gone out to do housework. There is no disgrace in being poor nor in honest work, but here in this semi southern society, a white girl who goes out to work is looked down upon, a mere servant. And it is very hard to a sensitive mind. And Ed it is hard for me to have to let my girls go out to do menial labor for the enemies of our faith. If I were permitted to use all my time in some business pursuit, I would not do it. If my children could go and work with those who understood the situation and were in the faith, it would not be quite so bad. But enough of this, Vida has written numerous applications for places in her line, (millinery) but has failed so far, and is making the best of it, and has gone out at service. . . . I will try Bro Dancer about the loan on the farm. Ed if I cannot do some thing soon I must abandon the idea of living in my own home.

—Alexander H. Smith, Letter to E. L. Kelley, May 30, 1883, P58-1, f1.

I am constantly reminded of my delinquencies and know not the day when the crash will come. And I be told "I cant carry you any longer."

—Alexander H. Smith, Letter, to E. L. Kelley, September 27, 1883, P16, f3, CofC Archives.

Though appointed by the church, Alex, along with other RLDS missionaries received minimal financial assistance from the church. During the early years of the Reorganization, missionaries were self sustaining. They provided for their own families while absent. Local jurisdictions provided missionaries in the field with food, housing, and sometimes assistance with travel. In the 1870s, the church bishop began providing the families of those appointed by the general church with limited support while they were in the field. This made it possible for Alexander to stay in the field for extended periods. But it was never enough. The family was falling behind.

By late 1884, Alexander's financial condition bordered upon the impossible. The family was saddled with mortgages on the farm in northern Missouri and their home in Independence. The Smiths were overextended and living on credit. Alex confided in the church bishop:

I am anxious about that mortgage on my place in Independence. It worries my wife, I wish it could be arranged some way. I wrote a letter while on board the ship and expressed myself somewhat then. It may be I can borrow the money and release the home but I think it doubtful.

—Alexander H. Smith, Letter to E. L. Kelley, Irvington, Alameda County, California, January 5, 1885, P16, f9, CofC Archives.

California, 1884-85

Joseph Smith III accompanied Alexander to California in 1885.

little bustle and irritation as could have well been done by anyone. He moved quickly about the house, but quietly, and there was seldom any apparent hurry and never needless words or excitement. He knew what he wanted to pack and how he wanted it packed and proceeded to do it, only asking to be undisturbed. He usually knew where to put his hand on what he wished to take with him. His one disturbing characteristic being his big, soft heart that felt keenly the pain and sorrow of parting and the anxiety of separation.

—"Biography of Patriarch Alexander Hale Smith," (October 1913) 407.

THE RLDS CONFERENCE sent Alexander back to California in both 1884 and 1885. His daughter Vida recalled his stoic approach to his missionary duties:

This constant travel was not always pleasant, but I think Father put as much or more pleasure into it than would the majority of men of his age and inclinations. It appeared to me that he made his preparations for departure as quietly and with as

During his August 1885 journey to California, Alexander traveled with Joseph III as far as Utah. Joseph then returned east. Alexander went on to California where he stayed for six months.

While in Oakland, Alexander boarded with the George and Emily Bartholomew family.

—Alexander H. Smith, Letter to W. H. Kelley, January 16, 1886, William H. Kelley Papers, P1, box 6, f9, item 1, 2, 3, 4, CofC Archives.

Vida's Marriage

Vida Elizabeth Smith.

Heman C. Smith.

WHILE ALEXANDER was far from home, a letter arrived from a young RLDS missionary, Heman C. Smith (no relation to Alexander), asking the hand of Alex's and Elizabeth's first-born daughter, Vida, in marriage. Alex extended a father's blessing to this union, with a mixture of joy and sadness.

Oakland Cal March 18th 1886
Heman C. Smith
Dear Brother
I received yours of March 9th on Monday and must admit I was surprised though not wholy [sic] so, for I have felt impressed that the crisis was near. I intuitively knew you re-garded my daughter with the highest esteem if not love. And confess I have been drawn towards you on that account though Vida has never even hinted at feelings other than those a sister might feel toward a brother. Bro Heman, Vida is like the apple of my eye to me. She is a child of the covenant. I don't know if you understand me or not, but to me she is all a child of promise can be. A bond given of God. She combines the love I had for my mother, and that I have for my child. I would never forget, I fear I could never forgive the man who ill treats her. Her happiness in common with that of my other children is nearest my heart. I would not have answered your letter so soon, but today there

came letters from my wife and Vida. My wife pleading your cause, and the happiness of our child.

I appreciate your worth, will make no eulogies on character, nor past history, but simply say in giving my consent, and with it my daughter, and parental blessing, it is all I can give, and still in thus giving I think I am giving into your keeping one of the purest and carest [dearest] gems this world holds. And oh Heman see to it, before God that you keep it undimmed and pure as your future happiness and hers also depends on the mutual bond being kept always unsullied and pure.

I do not write this without tears, for, I feel how I have leaned upon my Vida in my home life. And I forsee [sic] how hard it will be to give her up, but she assures me her happiness will be secured by the union. So take her my boy, and with her take a Fathers blessing. May the God of our fathers bless the union. May his Spirit be and abide with my children thus made one. And the holy angel of peace dwell with you now and evermore, in the name of Christ Jesus, our Lord, Amen. I remain as ever. Yours in double bonds

Alex Hale Smith
—Alexander H. Smith, Letter to Heman C. Smith, Oakland, California, March 18, 1886, P13, f330, CofC Archives.

Alex returned home in March 1886. After Vida's wedding, the new couple moved to California where Heman served as a RLDS missionary.

Joseph F. Smith

ALEXANDER PASSED through Salt Lake City on his return trip. He recalled, while preaching,

[Joseph F. Smith] arose and asked permission to speak. Of course I granted him liberty, and he . . . [bore] his testimony to Polig and charged his father and my father with being Polig's and with lying in their published testimony against it. . . . I told J.F.S. . . . [I] was heartily ashamed of him to stand before that immense congregation and proclaim his father a liar. . . .

—Alexander H. Smith, Letter to Edmund L. Kelley, December 19, 1883, P58-8, f1, CofC Archives.

Liberty Jail,
Liberty, Missouri

FOLLOWING Alexander's California trip, in 1886, he and Joseph III toured the remains of Liberty Jail, in Missouri, where their father had been incarcerated during the winter of 1838-39.

Aunt Katharine Salisbury

Alexander H. Smith, Sibian Wyman Salisbury, Mary Salisbury (Hancock) Dean, Don Carlos Salisbury, Emma Hale Salisbury, Fritz, (dog), Albert Salisbury, Grace Salisbury, Florence Salisbury, Herbert Salisbury, and Katharine Smith Salisbury.

ALEX REGULARLY MADE time for family, visiting his Aunt Katharine Salisbury at Fountain Green, Hancock County, Illinois, in 1886.

Ongoing Financial Concerns

ALEX KEPT RLDS Presiding Bishop E. L. Kelley updated about his financial circumstances. Nearing the end of hope, Alex received financial assistance from his California friend, George Bartholomew.

I receive a letter from Prof Geo Bartholomew today and he says I can draw on him for amount of incumbrance [sic] on this place, and give him a mortgage for three years, at six per cent interest. I can sell the place for $2000.00 but it is said to be worth $2500.00, I am now thinking of seeding down the farm and moving my family onto it next spring. If I sold now I would have no place to live till my tenant left the farm. Shall sell this place between now and next conference, am going to labor this year in the ministry, and do the best I can and if the screws dont let up, next spring will quietly crawl in a hole, and pull the hole in after me.

—Alexander H. Smith, Independence, Missouri, Letter to E. L. Kelley, May 6, 1886, P16, f13, CofC Archives.

Physical and financial stresses began to affect Elizabeth's health. Alex wrote:

Edmund L. Kelley.

My wifes [sic] health is poor she seems on the eve of loosing her hearing altogether, her head troubles her very much. She has received nothing on her allowance this nor last month, and the expenses of living still goes on. What the Bishop gave me at Lamoni of course has been used for living perposes [sic]. I have been offered two chances for work, but I cant, I positively can't allow the effect of my quitting the field to come upon the church.

—Alexander H. Smith, Independence, Missouri, Letter to E. L. Kelley, May 6, 1886, P16, f13, CofC Archives.

In the end, Alex realized he could no longer remain in the mission field and sustain his family in Independence, Missouri. So, the Smiths executed a deed of trust with George Bartholomew, of Oakland, California, and John W. Brackenbury, of Independence, Missouri, using the Smiths' farm in northern Missouri as collateral. Alex signed a three-year promissory note and paid off the mortgage on his Independence home.

In 1887 the RLDS Conference convened at Kirtland, Ohio. Though Alex was president of the Quorum of Twelve, he could not afford to attend. Instead, he made plans to move his family back to the farm at Andover, Missouri. He wrote to a fellow member of the Twelve, William H. Kelley:

Independence Mo. Mar 11th 87
Elder Wm H. Kelley
   Kirtland Ohio
Your welcome missive came to hand this morning, was thinking of you yesterday and wondering why you had not written.

Got a card from J R Lambert yesterday, saying if his health will permit he intends being at Con.

I am in a quandary as to the necessity of my being there. Am not in financial condition to come, and unless my superiors order it, shall not come. I am expected to retrench, am trying to do so. Shall make out my report and send it up, also report to the Quo. Am tired of being the standing grumbler, so will set down.

Joseph says he knows of no urgent necessity of my going but upon general principles thinks I ought.

Bring my family to conference or any of them? Not much. I asked the Bishop once for $10.00 to take Vida my eldest daughter to general Conce I didn't get it "thought I better not incur the expense." It would be establishing a bad "Precedent," Bah!

No it will cost me between $40.00 and $50.00 to attend Conce this spring and I have'nt got it to spare. Board $4.00 a week, 2 weeks $8.00. Fare to Cleveland $21.40 to Willowby 90 cts to Kirtland 25 cts and return will make a bill of some $53.10 not counting incidentals and I cant afford to do it as I have been told, I have no claim outside of what is allowed to my family, and I do not choose to use their support.

Yes I am making preparation to move, shall likely move next week. What think you will it be necessary for me or rather our quo to be at the coming Conce? Can we do anything if we are there?

It will take all I can rake and scrape to move me. I tell you "Hope" does not shine very brightly before me now.

But then its all right I guess, I am agoing to quit grunting and stand it just as long as I can and then kick like a mule.

Ed owes me a letter. He's gone over too, and is too busy to give me a few minutes sass.

I shall see Joseph tomorrow or next day, and can tell better what to do after a talk with him, he comes to dedicate the Armstrong Chapel.

Joseph Luff comes to conference in the interest of our new Chapel here, he had an increase in his family this morning, a boy.

My family are in moderate health. Give my regards to ELKs folks and all the Saints. With kind remembrance to your family. I am as ever

Alex Hale Smith

—Alexander H. Smith, Letter to W. H. Kelley, March 11, 1887, William H. Kelley Papers, P1, box 8, f1, items 13, 14, CofC Archives.

Alex addressed his circumstances further with the church bishop.

Independence, Mo, Mar 20th 1887
Bro E L Kelley

Your missive of 17th inst is at hand. Our expectations are doomed to disappointment in this life. Am not now in pos[s]ession of wisdom enough to say whether I can come to con[feren]ce or not. You may not see my Phiz [physiognomy] at Kirtland, and again you may. We are having the measles at our house, and I have sold my home here and will have to move, as soon as the measles depart.

As to those Utah Elders. They lie from A to Izard. The only ground they can have for their tale, is that certain women was sent to our meeting instructed to bear their testimony if we said anything about Polig. They came to the meeting, but kept their mouths shut. I had been informed of their object and was ready to meet them, and prove them to be liars. It was Davids [day to] preach . . . and he held them spell bound to the finish, with tears in their eyes. That was when David and I were there. We were introduced to them by Wm Huntington or Dimock Huntington, I think the former, but no word on the matter of Father and Poligamy [sic].

If they tell more than this they speak falsely. Joseph can answer for himself. I know of nothing of the sort, in his case. Will writes me I will be needed Joseph says I ought to go and I feel so myself, but the expense is a w[r]e[c]k in the way. I have said nothing about the relative cost of coming this way or going that way, to conference between you and I, but simply say I do not feel disposed to take the amount neces[s]ary to come from amount allowed my family. And will not do it. When I was down and asked the church to help me up, they would not do it, for fear of establishing a bad "precedent." All right, I propose to count the cost, in the future, before rushing into the fight. I'm not going to war any more without first counting costs to see if I can pay the shot. A wise builder counts the cost before he begins to build. I am a poor scholar if I do not learn by experience. And my past has not been so pleasant in a financial point of view as to cause me to fall in love with it, nor was my effort to get expenses paid, so flattering that I should run without tidings to incur other expense, so much for the financial "situation." While I realize my obligations to the church I have others jest as binding and although by the strictest economy my family and self managed to get through the passed 12 months without falling behind. We have gained nothing to pay back debts, so are compelled to sell our home here and remove to a less expensive place to live, and while

I do not intend to quit the ministry I do intend to retrench, and if so be it I shall be the will of God I will sleep once more, a free man ere I die out of debt.

I expect to go to Lamoni this week and prepare my house on the farm for the tribe of Alex, and hence forth eat clover and browse for a living. How is that for high?

I may possibly come on to Kirtland with Joseph, by the way he too thinks the church ought to bear expense of my coming. But its a bad precedent, you know, if my expense is paid, someone else will claim that theirs also ought to be. D'ye see?

Well Ed this is a queer world eh! There is a strong feeling against my leaving Indce by all the st. [saints] here, Joseph dont like it at all, but I could not get out of bondage otherwise. Give my regards to all, your family in particular. I never moved in my life feeling as "perfectly awful" about as I do about my contemplated move this time.

Yours Alex Hale Smith

—Alexander H. Smith, Letter, E. L. Kelley, Independence, Missouri, March 20, 1887, P16, f15, CofC Archives.

Independence, Missouri, Church Building

Members of the RLDS Independence, Missouri, Brick Church priesthood, and Alex and Elizabeth, Independence, ca. 1885.

WHILE LIVING IN INDEPENDENCE, the Alexander Smith family fellowshipped with the Independence RLDS branch in a small brick church building on East Lexington Avenue. Alexander, along with others advocated the erection of a more suitable place of worship. The branch began planning to construct a substantial building of limestone near the Independence Temple Lot on West Lexington.

Emma Belle's Wedding

Death of William Anderson

TO ALEX'S SORROW, his friend and former missionary companion, William Anderson, died unexpectedly in the spring of **1888.** Alexander remembered William, saying: "There are remembrances delightful to recall of God's richest and wonderful feasts spread for them by his spirit as they journeyed together binding in bonds of friendship and love to the gospel and each other for life."

SOON AFTER the family relocated back to the farm, the wedding of their daughter Emma Belle (eighteen years old) to William Kennedy (twenty-four) occurred on October 5, 1887.

—"Biography of Patriarch Alexander Hale Smith," (July 1913) 309.

—Daisy Bowen Brown, Letter, October 1, 1947, P43-1, f1, CofC Archives; William Anderson, Obituary, "Died," *Herald* 35, no. 12 (March 24, 1888): 191.

Stone Church Dedication

Independence, Missouri, Stone Church cornerstone dedication, 1888.

EARLY IN 1888, ALEX returned to Independence to participate in the cornerstone-laying ceremony for the Stone Church. Vida recalled:

I met my father at the annual [1888] spring Conference, held that year at Independence, Missouri. On April sixth of that year the cornerstone of the Stone church at that place was laid with becoming ceremonies. Father was one of the speakers on that occasion, and father "making his talk" he came around to where I stood and took

my year-old boy and held him during the remainder of the ceremonies. The other incidents of that day seem very dim to me today, but looking back . . . I fancy I see him press the little form of my boy close to him, his face radiant with living emotions and his eyes lighting with pride and delight, his hat held in his hand left his dark hair tossing in the cool, spring wind.

—"Biography of Patriarch
Alexander Hale Smith,"
(October 1913) 394.

Mission Field

THE APRIL 1888 RLDS Conference placed Alexander in charge of the large north central mission field. Part of his mission included Clitherall, Minnesota, where a large concentration of followers of Alpheus Cutler lived. By the time of Alexander's visit, many of Cutler's disciples had affiliated with the RLDS Church. Though pleased with the condition of the work in that area, Alex poured out his financial concerns to Bishop Edmund L. Kelley.

FOLLOWING conference, Vida visited her parents at the farm.

"It was during this visit home that my sister [Ina] and myself accompanied Father on some of his preaching trips in the 'regions round about,' assisting him with our faith and songs." Vida could never think of that time without picturing her "father standing in some weather-beaten, cheerless old schoolhouse, spreading a royal spiritual feast for a few straggling but earnest hearers."

—"Biography of Patriarch Alexander Hale Smith," (October 1913) 396.

Clitherall Minn Aug 4th 1888
Bro E L Kelley

. . . The work is fairly good throughout most of my large field as reported to me.

I guess I will have to get you to help me out of a scrape I have got into financially in the effort I had to make in leaving Independence.

I borrowed seven hundred dols of Bro Geo Bartholomew to release that city property so I could sell it and give a mortgage on my farm home where I now live calculating to pay Bro B out of the proceeds of sale, but was forced to make improvements which took my nest egg

Alexander H. Smith, ca. 1886.

Edmund L. Kelley, RLDS Presiding Bishop.

so I am now flat and only one more year to raise the money. Do you know of any way I can get the riches to meet the claim? I never can do it while I remain in the field. Last year the church did well by me and lifted some of my trouble. I cannot ask any thing from that direction, and yet I see in the future the sure loss of my home if I cannot make some turn to raise the wind. And so it goes, Ed I fear you will say. Its the same old doleful cry and whine. Well so be it, you are the only man I have said any thing to about it of late and if you see a ray of light for me point it out, my good boy, and give me the benefit of your financial foresight.

My family was well when last heard from. Ina went home with Vida, and is now in Cal. Our home seems more lonely since the girls and young Heman left us. If you write soon direct to this place care [of] J.R. Anderson.

With kind regards to all and love to Kelley and the Kelleys. I remain yours in Christ.

Alex Hale Smith

—Alexander H. Smith, Clitherall, Minnesota, Letter to Edmund L. Kelley, August 4, 1888, P16, f16, CofC Archives.

Description, 1890

VIDA DESCRIBED HER **father as he appeared around 1890:**

Father had grown very portly, but his health was much better than in earlier years. When sister Ina came from California, where she had been for a few years with me, she wrote me, "I was tired and the crowd was great in the city, but suddenly I found myself in the arms of a portly gentleman and felt all my worry and weariness roll away." It was always like a tonic to meet Father in the midst of confusion and weariness and irritating crowds. He was so sure and easy and comfortable, and we felt a sort of pride in being thus companioned and chaperoned. And this feeling was not confined alone to his own daughters. His nieces felt the same loving care and tenderness and chivalry from him.

—"Biography of Patriarch Alexander Hale Smith," (October 1913) 403.

Move *to* Lamoni, Iowa

Alexander H. Smith house, Lamoni, Iowa, ca. 1900. Courtesy Gracia Jones.

AFTER A COUPLE OF years on the farm, Alexander extended his mortgage arrangement with George Barthomew and relocated his family to Lamoni, Iowa, in 1890. Alex's and Elizabeth's home was at 502 South Maple Street, near the campus of Graceland College.

Vida recalled:

It was during the winter days of 1890 that a trade was made in which the farm finally passed out of the family possession and a new home in Lamoni was dedicated by Father and Mother. Mother was happy. She had room for flowers and chickens and cows, and for Father a wide, fine garden and place for fruit; in fact all the comforts of a farm and also conveniences of a wide-awake town and none of the burdens of harvest and seedtime. Here Mother thought to spend her days until the sun set. The first beautiful incident of family life to consecrate the new home walls was the marriage of sister Ina to Mr. Sidney G. Wright of Australia, a marriage whose one element of sadness was the shadow of separation, for they went soon after to their Australian home and the years seemed very long to those left behind.

—"Biography of Patriarch Alexander Hale Smith," (October 1913) 404.

The land transaction provided some relief. Alex described it in a letter to Bishop E. L. Kelley, November 8, 1890:

I suppose you heard of my trade. I wish I could have seen you ere you left Lamoni. I wish your aid in arranging some plan to raise the needful to release my home from that mortgage. My trade does not release me, but gives me something I can sell, and get a part of the means to pay it, and still have a good home. I've thought you might think of some plan to relieve my wifes [sic] mind of the constant strain and help me. Do you know of any one who could spare five or six hundred for a few years, at small interest, and take my personal obligation?

I think I made a mistake when I objected to the proposition to lift my financial distress by contribution. If such a plan was proposed now I wouldn't refuse. I think it will come to that yet, or I will lose my home. And I think my wife would go crazy, if that should take place.

She has worked very hard to save it. And now she cannot do as she has done, and it is on her account largely, I make the change. Now Ed if you can think of any means to help me, write and let me hear it.

—Alexander H. Smith, Letter to Edmund L. Kelley, Andover, Missouri, November 8, 1890, Edmund L. Kelley Papers, P16, f25, CofC Archives.

Alex was a bit more forthcoming with his colleague William Kelley about the nature of his land dealings.

Bro Wm H Kelley
    Dear Sir
    . . . All goes well in my field so far as reported. I am at home. Have traded my farm for property in Lamoni, am now making arrangements for removal. My trade does not relieve me from my indebtedness but I think it places me in a better position to spend more time in the field.

Say Will cant you think of some plan to raise me some $500.00 or $600.00 and release my home from that mortgage put on it when I left Independence. It worries my wife sorely, and I am not free from anxiety.

I see no way of making any money while in the ministry and have no way out of it. So must simply wait until the close, and then lose all.

But perhaps providence intends it so, to keep me humble.

Do you know of anyone who has means enough to spare me the above amount and wait three or four years, at a small rate of interest.

What think you of "That Manifesto"? Is it not quite a come round? An easy way to justify oneself, to lay the responsibility on the shoulders of the national government. But unfortunately they do quote, that "Rev, Be obedient to the laws that be," given years before their pet Polig is claimed to have come.

Well, well, I hope they will learn obedience, if need be, by the things which they suffer.

It is storming here now, raining and freezing. This country is covered with ice. Today is the second one of the storm.

Its gloomy enough and I feel its influence. With kind regards to all I remain yours Resply
Alex Hale Smith

—Alexander H. Smith, Letter to W. H. Kelley, November 8, 1890, William H. Kelley Papers, P1, box 10, f8, item 8, CofC Archives.

Right: 1890 Conference attendees outside the Lamoni Brick Church, including: Apostles G. T. Griffith, J. H. Lake, W. H. Kelley, H. C. Smith, Bishop E. L. Kelley, and President Joseph Smith III. Below: Alexander H. Smith, ca. 1890.

1890 Conference

ON APRIL 8, DURING THE 1890 RLDS Conference at Lamoni, Iowa, Alexander was called by revelation to be the president of the Twelve. He was ordained by Joseph III and W. W. Blair to that office. Alex bore testimony of his call to the conference saying:

While traveling in southern California, in one period of my ministry, my surroundings were such that I was cast down in sprit, discouraged, worn and tired. I felt very much like giving up and going home. Retiring to rest I presented myself before the Lord. I asked him for some encouragement. During the night I received by the influence of the Spirit the following: I saw a city upon a hill. I saw to the eastward of the city a rolling prairie country. The city appeared to have walls. . . . I came to the east side of the city and seemed to be standing on the top of the wall. . . . On gazing toward the east I beheld a band of people approaching. They seemed to be led by one that was riding a horse and as they approached the city they came singing. I stood watching until they came near to the gate, and as they approached it the one that was leader alighted from his horse, and instead of going through the gate, came up the broad flight of steps and approached me. I recognized him and I cried out, "My father! O my father!" He took me in his arms and embraced me. He said, "Be cheered, be comforted; the time is near when your position will be changed; let your heart be comforted." I awoke, was filled with the spirit, and weeping.

—"Biography of A. H. Smith," *Journal of History* 6, no. 4 (October 1913): 400.

In addition to his new duties, Alexander continued his ministerial labors in local jurisdictions and at church reunions.

Nauvoo, Summer 1890

Alexander standing in Nauvoo Mansion doorway, 1890.

WHENEVER opportunity afforded, Alexander returned to Nauvoo for short visits. During the summer of 1890, Alex and Joseph III sadly determined that the dilapidated condition of the hotel wing threatened the survival of the Mansion House. Alexander's diary recorded: "[I] Let [a] contract [to Lyman Beecher] to tear down the [wing of the] old house." The remainder of the house was re-roofed and painted red.

Vida recalled,

In a letter written by Father to me in 1892, I find this reference to his work on the old Mansion, and photos taken of the place.

"The front view is the best, but a view from the east will show what I had done to the old home. I had to have all the big dining room and all east of the room where the brick oven was, torn down and of course the part thus exposed weatherboarded up, so it leaves the house as it was ere the addition was built. No. 9 [sic 10], the room you were born in, of course went with the rest. The house is a good house now. I had it newly roofed and painted red. George W. Dundee lives in it now. It looked real cozy and home-like when I was there last summer—made me almost homesick. I love the old place yet, and would gladly go back if there were Saints enough to form a church there; and I had means enough to fix up the old home as I would love to. I have purchased David's part of the lot and the two rooms that were left, so own the entire building now. It did look bunty for awhile after tearing the long part away. The floor of the big dining room was so rotten it was dangerous to walk over it, the roof on the north side had rotted and fallen in, in places. I could have cried if it would have done any good. The south side was in better preservation. Rooms 9, 10, and 7 were in a fair state except as the other part had settled and left the doors awry and the floors uneven. I would not stay to see it torn down; it was bad enough to see it after. So much for the old "house where you were born." Two of the pine trees Mother set out are still living; one at the corner rises above the housetop now, the one in front is not so tall. . . . Give my kind regards to those

Saints who so kindly remember me. Would love to see them, and those babies, God bless them. How I would love to see them and be Santa Claus to them indeed! They should have their cars and dolls and boxes, too, if I were there and able. When I think of the grandchildren, ah, then it is hard to be poor.

Talk about the homesick heartsick, away from home, among comparative strangers. But I am in good quarters and every wish forestalled in a manner. Brother Green and family are kindness itself, but I am hungry to see my own loved ones. I want a kiss, a loving caress. Don't you know a loving caress from one we love is better than medicine, and your foolish old father is nearly starving for the little mother and his loving girls; but pshaw, I must stop or I'll make you homesick, too. Kiss those darlings for Grandpa.

—"Biography of Patriarch Alexander Hale Smith," (October 1913) 401-2.

Rear view of Mansion House hotel wing.

Administrator

Joseph III in his office at Lamoni, Iowa. Richard S. Salyards, church secretary, (center) and Alexander (right).

BETWEEN CHURCH-related trips, Alexander used the time to attend to administrative duties. In this photograph, he is shown sitting in Joseph Smith III's office in the Herald publishing plant building with R. S. Salyards, in 1890.

While giving a 1900 Conference talk, probably in reference to the work in California, Alexander gratefully noted: "Our advance has been . . . slow, seemingly, but it has been sure. We have not had to yield any ground where we have planted ourselves."

—A. H. Smith, 1900 Conference talk, *Journal of History*, 7, no. 1 (January 1914): 63.

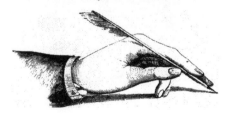

Smith Family Burial Ground Marker

Standing Left: Joseph III, Alex's son Frederick A. Smith, Alexander H. Smith, and J. T. Ponce. Sitting: Joe Salyards, 1891.

AT THE TIME OF Lewis Bidamon's funeral in 1891, the family finally erected a modest marker upon Emma's grave. Joseph III hired H. H. Hudson, of Nauvoo, to purchase and set a stone monument upon a brickwork base.

Following Bidamon's funeral, Alexander and Joseph posed for photographs next to the Homestead.

Emma Smith Bidamon Grave Marker.

RLDS Church Leaders, 1892

ALEXANDER WAS an apostle from 1873 to 1897 and served as president of the Quorum of Twelve from 1890 to 1897. This composite picture of members of the Twelve was produced and offered to RLDS Church members for purchase around 1892.

Eva Grace *and* Monty

Eva Grace Smith Madison.

LaMonte (Monty) Madison. Images courtesy of Gracia Jones.

ALEXANDER'S daughter, Eva Grace, married Forest Lamont Madison, in 1891. The Madisons made their home in San Bernardino, California, where Eva Grace died on March 18, 1892, after giving birth to a son, LaMonte.

—Anderson, *Ancestry and Posterity of Joseph Smith and Emma Hale* (Independence, Missouri: Herald Publishing House, 1929), 598.

Eva's husband, Forest Lamont Madison, was unable to provide for the baby. So Alexander's wife, Elizabeth, travelled to California by train and brought baby Monty home to Lamoni. There, Alexander's family cared for the boy until he was about sixteen years old. Monty's was a rather sad and difficult life. But he always carried a tender spot in his heart for his grandmother Elizabeth.

—Thanks to Gracia Jones.

Nauvoo House's Future

Charlie Bidamon became the owner of the Nauvoo House (Riverside Mansion) following Lewis Bidamon's 1891 death.

LEARNING THAT THE **Nauvoo House would be changing hands, Alex encouraged RLDS Bishop Kelley to secure the building for the church.**

Chicago Ills May 31st 1893

Bro E L Kelley

In visiting Nauvoo I learned that the site of the Nauvoo House in fact the whole block is to be sold at auction, Administrators sale, on the 17th day of June, at the door of the Post Office Nauvoo. Dont you think it would be a good move for the church to buy it? It is historic ground and might be a crum of vantage ground, in the near future.

The indebtedness of the estate, I learned is about $125.00 The probabilities are the place will not bring much, at a forced sale for cash. It may reach $500.00 costs and all, what think you?

Had an effort better be made to redeem the "waste place"? And hold it preparatory to the rebuilding of that corner stone.

I cant buy it, and I've written to Joseph and he says he cant. I believe it would be a good time to get the property cheap, and if I had time I could raise the money by subscription. But there comes in the question will it bring in anything as an income to pay the interest on the money invested until it will be needed? I am forced to say I see no way of making it do so now, but I hate to see it pass into the hands of strangers.

Shall remain here till the first of next week. What is Bro Peters address? We had a very pleasant time at the mission.

I wonder if I couldnt inveigle ex Bishop Rogers to invest that 500.00 he saved? I have a good mind to write him anyway. I dont know why it is. I havent for years felt a particle of interest in the old place until of late, I feel impressed we ought to take advantage of every opportunity to get a foot hold there again.

If I had the money to spare (I feel now) I would risk five hundred on it if need be anyhow.

Write me what you think of it. Am not feeling first class but am not sick, had a little trouble with heart monday [sic] morning, which left me feeling very tired.

With regards to all.

I am very Resfly,

Alex Hale Smith

742 Clybourn Ave, Chicago Ills

—Alexander H. Smith, Chicago, Illinois, Letter, to Edmund L. Kelley, May 31, 1893, P54, f47, CofC Archives.

Reunion, 1896

Alexander and aunt, Katharine Salisbury, with RLDS leaders posed at Bluff Park Reunion, Burlington, Iowa, in 1896, to commemorate the semi-centennial of the exodus from Nauvoo.

Presidency

Alexander, standing, with RLDS First Presidency; William W. Blair, and Joseph Smith III, ca. 1895.

ALEXANDER remained in the Twelve through 1897 when he was called into the First Presidency. He served as Joseph III's counselor until 1902.

Presiding Evangelist

ON HIS DEATHBED IN September 1840, Joseph Smith Sr. called [for] his son Hyrum and ordained him as his successor.

—H. Michael Marquardt, comp., *Early Patriarchal Blessings of The Church of Jesus Christ of Latter-day Saints* (Salt Lake City: The Smith-Pettit Foundation, 2007), xiii.

This created a precedent that

the presiding patriarchate operated outside of the control of the church's First Presidency and was a privilege held by right of lineage within the Smith family.

—John Hamer, "Review of H. Michael Marquardt, comp., *Early Patriarchal Blessings of The Church of Jesus Christ of Latter-day Saints*"(Salt Lake City: The Smith-Pettit Foundation, 2007), *The John Whitmer Historical Association*

Journal, 28 (2008): 305.

Joseph III allowed the office of RLDS Presiding Evangelist/Patriarch to remain vacant during the lifetime of his uncle William B. Smith. In 1897, Alexander accepted the position. The church provided him with a secretary.

As this was a new ministry in the Reorganization, Alexander had to develop his own patriarchal methodology. His task was materially aided by the skill of a young man named Leon Arthur Gould (1876-1971) who became Alexander's close associate in this evangelical ministry. Gould was

Leon Gould, courtesy Roland Sarratt.

born in Minnesota, May 7, 1876. He served as Alexander's stenographer, recording blessings. More than this, Leon became Alexander's trusted companion, who accompanied Alex everywhere. Gould came to be referred to as "Alexander's shadow." In later life, Gould served as associate editor of the RLDS Church young adult oriented periodical, *Autumn Leaves,* and later the RLDS Church periodical *Saints' Herald.* During his tenure as editor, Leon was ordained a high priest in the RLDS Church, June 18, 1905.

The following is a sample of the wording from one of Alexander's patriarchal blessings:

Do not lose faith in thy fellows of like covenant with thee. Remember that humanity is weak, and remember that each one sees this latter day work from the standpoint that they occupy, and sometimes what thou cant not see, thy brother or thy sister may see to an advantage. Sometimes what they see thou canst not see. Sometimes what thou seest they can not behold. Remember this; and that the line of sentinels to see eye to eye must be so arranged that each can see that part of the work over which they have care, and they are placed in trust. If they will watch that part over which they are placed in trust, faithfully, and do their part, it does not matter what others may do, they will receive their reward. So it is with thee. Fill the niche in the great work which God has established in this latter day, in which He has placed thee by reason of thy creation, by reason of the providences which He has thrown around thee, by reason of the very troubles and distresses that have come to thee in consequence of this latter day work. . . . I seal upon thee, in the name of the Lord Jesus, the promise of Eternal Life. The right is thine. Thou has sought to obtain it, and if faithful it shall be given thee in joy and peace and honor and in contentment in the Kingdom of God, where thou shall reign over the sphere of action granted thee, living with those who shall be redeemed, brought into the presence of our Lord and Savior, to dwell upon the earth in its redeemed condition.

—Alexander H. Smith, Evangelist's Blessing of Abbie Horton, 1903, Smith Papers, P70-1, f8, CofC

Evangelist Visits

ALEXANDER VISITED many local jurisdictions and reunions as Presiding

Evangelist/Patriarch. Alexander posed with local leaders at the 1897 Boston Reunion.

Boston, Massachusetts, Reunion, 1897. Front: Joseph Luff, Alexander H. Smith, and Edmund L. Kelley

On an ongoing basis, from 1897 to 1902, when Joseph III was out of the office, Alexander assisted with the Presidency's correspondence. Alex's letters of this period address complex issues of church polity and law, such as matters involving divorce and remarriage, and ordination irregularities.

—Alexander H. Smith Letterbook, 1897-1901, MS 17756, LDS Church Library.

Cousin Fred

Frederick V. Salisbury, son of Katharine Smith Salisbury, ca. 1870s.

ALEXANDER addressed the following remarkable letter to his cousin Fred Salisbury. This document affords an unvarnished view of Alexander's core religious sentiments, giving insights into the theological understandings and grounded faith that guided Alexander's life of extraordinary commitment and sacrifice.

Written in part at Lamoni, Iowa, June 2, 1897, finished at Blue Rapids, Kansas, June 5. 1897.

Lamoni, Iowa June 2nd 1897
Cousin Fred Salisbury

Bro. Joseph was kind enough to show me a letter from you today, in which you ask some questions, which I may aid you in understanding, but to do so I will examine some of the foundation upon which the Reorganized Church of Jesus Christ of L.D.S. is built.

There is no need of calling your attention to proofs of the mission of Joseph Smith the Martyr. My Father and your Uncle. But some of the revelations through him to the church have never been understood, or else have been willfully misrepresented, and misinterpreted. I shall take my own way to reach your question and answer it, Joseph will also answer you, or at least he said he would. Bro. Richard Salyard[s] sent you some tracts which contain much valuable matter and are to be relied upon. You may depend upon the quotations used as correct, the books quoted can all be seen here in Herald office. And now for my examination of Gods word to support the claim of my Bro. Joseph, as successor of Joseph the Martyr. His statement in the matter will

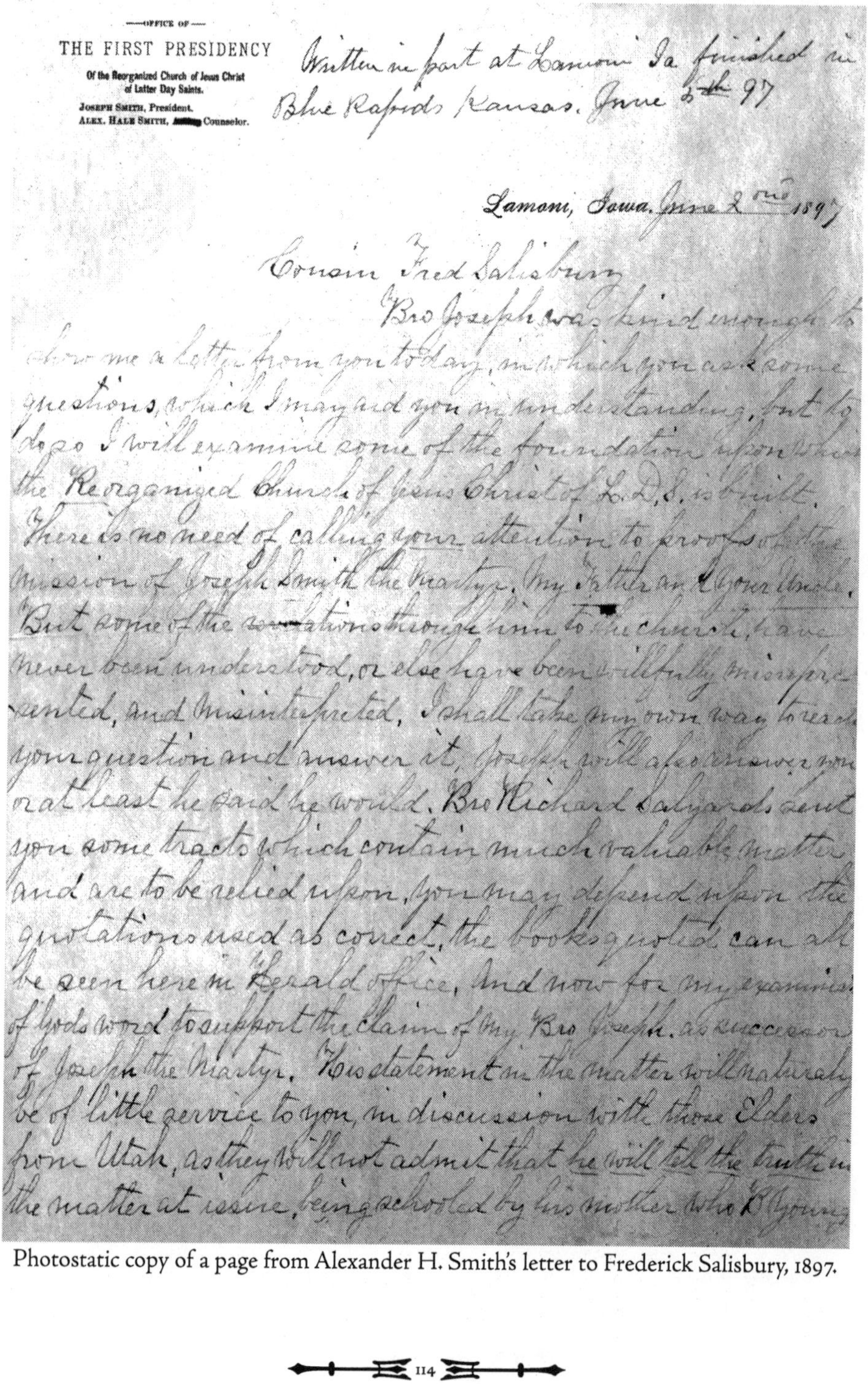

—OFFICE OF—

THE FIRST PRESIDENCY

Of the Reorganized Church of Jesus Christ
of Latter Day Saints.

JOSEPH SMITH, President.
ALEX. HALE SMITH, Counselor.

Written in part at Lamoni Ia. finished in
Blue Rapids Kansas. June 2 97

Lamoni, Iowa. June 2ⁿᵈ 1897

Cousin Fred Salisbury

Bro Joseph was kind enough to
show me a letter from you today, in which you ask some
questions, which I may aid you in understanding, but to
do so I will examine some of the foundation upon which
the Reorganized Church of Jesus Christ of L.D.S. is built.
There is no need of calling your attention to proofs of the
mission of Joseph Smith the Martyr. My Father and your Uncle.
But some of the revelations through him to the church, have
never been understood, or else have been willfully misrepresented, and misinterpreted, I shall take my own way to read
your question and answer it, Joseph will also answer you
or at least he said he would. Bro Richard Salyards sent
you some tracts which contain much valuable matter
and are to be relied upon, you may depend upon the
quotations used as correct, the books quoted can all
be seen here in Herald office, And now for my examination
of Gods word to support the claim of my Bro Joseph, as successor
of Joseph the Martyr, His statement in the matter will naturally
be of little service to you, in discussion with those Elders
from Utah, as they will not admit that he will tell the truth in
the matter at issue, being schooled by his mother who B Young

Photostatic copy of a page from Alexander H. Smith's letter to Frederick Salisbury, 1897.

natural[l]y be of little service to you, in discussion with those Elders from Utah, as they will not admit that <u>he will tell the truth</u> in the matter at issue, being schooled by his mother who B Young Said was the "Damndest Liar that ever lived," and those fellows will simply ignore anything which Joseph or I may say on the history of the church, for that reason I take the present mode of answering you for your good.

What I refer to in the revelations is the plain provision made for just, what occurred, that is the taking away the Prophet. I call your attention, first to Sec 2 Par 4 of Book of D. Covenants, and there is the plain statement, to the Prophet, "because of transgression if thou art not aware thou wilt fall, but remember God is merciful." I quote this to show that the Prophet was not infal[l]ible, but might do wrong. It is so often quoted, "What the Prophet Joseph did was right, and we have no right to question what he did." And also to show a foreshaddowing of evil to come to the Prophet. And again Sec 4 Par 4, God says, "I command you my servant Joseph to repent and walk more upright[ly] before me and yield to the persuasions of men no more and that you be firm in keeping the commandments wherewith I have commanded you, and if you do this, behold I grant unto

you eternal life, even if you should be slain."

Notice here Coz Fred, God foreshaddows the fact that he would be slain and father for a long time understood it so. Now see if God knew the Prophet would be taken, it is but reasonable to believe he would provide for his church in such an emergency, and we believe he did, as I will endeavor to show. It has always seemed strange to me with the bible book of mormon and doctrine and covenants in their hands how so many were led astray. For nothing is more clearly established in the restoration, in this latter day work than, the law of lineal decent [sic] in the right to the priesthood. It is one of the pillars upon which the work rests.

They can no more get away from the decrees of God as pertaining to the lineal right to the priesthood, and presidency, than they can escape the Gospel law of condemnation, if they do wrong, and reject the truth. Rev. Sec 83. Par 1-2 & 3 and Sec 84, Par 3, the latter reads. "Therefore thus saith the Lord unto you. (Who? Why Joseph to whom he is talking) with whom the priesthood hath continued, through the lineage of your fathers, for ye are lawful heirs according to the (promise?) (no) the flesh, and have been hid from the world with Christ in

God, therefore your life (not lives) and the priesthood hath remained and must needs remain through your lineage until the restitution of all things &c and again Sec 107 Par 18, where the Lord says the blessings of Joseph is put upon the head of his posterity after him (which is the present Joseph). Now I take up the line again and show just how nicely the revelations confirm Josephs calling. Sec 23, Par 4 is this promise. "Be patient in afflictions for thou shalt have many; but endure them, for lo, I am with you (Joseph Father) even unto the end of thy days. ("Even if you should be slain Sec 4-4.")

You notice here is seemingly an unconditioned promise to the end of the mortal life of the Prophet. God knew he would remain faithful, but he also knew he would be taken away from the church, so he provides for it. In Sec 27 Par 2. God says "I have given him the keys of the mysteries and revelations, which are sealed, until I shall appoint unto them (the church) another in his stead. Note the keys of the mysteries of the revelations are given to Joseph the Prophet, until he God should appoint unto them. Who? the church another. Note again the Keys are given to Joseph not to the 12 and he was to hold them, how long? let us see. Sec 64, Par 2. "and the keys of the mysteries of the

kingdom, shall not be taken from my servant Joseph Smith Jr through the means I have appointed while he liveth. &c. See Sec 87 Par 2. "Verily I say unto you (Joseph) the keys of this kingdom shall never be taken from you while thou art in this world neither in the world to come. Nevertheless through you shall the oracles (or revelations) be given to another yea even unto the church." The idea that Fathers mantle fell on Brigham is all nonsense, devilish nonsense. See again as pertaining to the keys father held towards the 12. Sec 105, Par 6. "Rebel not against my Joseph Servant Joseph, for verily I say unto you I am with him, and my hand shall be over him and the keys which I have given unto him and also to youward. Shall not be taken from him till I come."

Now Fred, What conclusion must we come to? God said if the Seer should be taken he God would appoint another in his stead, but he would do it through him, his chosen Seer. See Sec 43 Par 2. You will see there, God further explains, and says. None else shall be appointed unto his gift except it be through him. &c and then goes on to say. "For verily I say unto (the church) that he that is ordained of me shall come in at the gate, and be ordained["] as I have told you before, to teach those revelations which you have received and shall receive through him whom I have appointed.

Now I think I have quoted enough to make the matter plain. God tells us, the Seer will be taken, that he will not lose his keys, and gifts, that God will appoint another in his stead, this indicates that his successor will not take his place while he the seer lives. Also that the one God had ordained must come in at the Gate, meaning baptism, note God seems to have "ordained before" some one. Now who is it? God never forgets himself, nor his law, so he remembers the lineage he has watched over so many hundred years and makes his appointment according. In the summer of 1843 while a large concourse of people stood on the banks of the grand old Mississippi river watching a baptism, as the Prophet comes out of the water having immersed the last who had given their name, he lifts his voice and crys, "Is there any one else wishes to give themselves to the service of God. Now is the accepted time" from a group of boys near the outskirts of the concourse of people, comes the answer, "here I am father I do." And the lad God had ordained, threw his hat behind him and ran forward to be led through the gate. As God said he shall come in at the gate. And through my servant Joseph will I appoint him. The

lad was confirmed and subsequently was called before the council in the upper chamber of the brick store and annointed [sic] and blessed. Now all this was foreshaddowed [sic] by the events occurring in Missouri and by prophecy, but it would take too long to tell it now suffice it to say in the jail at Liberty Mo. Father put his hands on the head of Joseph his son, and Prophiticaly [sic] blessed him, and in his annointing [sic] at Nauvoo, the blessing of his Father was put upon his head, and it was so announced upon the stand in Nauvoo, but now as to the claim that he was ordained by father to fill his place. Father could hardly do that while he lived that is his place could not be occupied but by him while he lived, he did it so far as was possible in the blessing and setting apart to the prophetic calling. Now you ask why was it necessary for him to be ordained by Bro Marks. See Sec 17, Par 17. "Every president of the high priesthood &c is to be ordained by direction of a high council of general conference." This is the law, and God did not choose to ignore it, he gave it, and so he would comply with it, hence ordered, Josephs going where he had a servant who could ordain according to the law. A vote of a general conference was had, and Joseph was ordained by William Marks, president of the high priesthood, of the high council of the corner stake of Zion, Nauvoo at the time of the death of the Prophet.

Cousin Fred there is no clearer line of authority given in all the hand dealing of God in all the ages past than that of the present Josephs [sic]. He was ordained a high priest an apostle, president of the high priesthood, and so accepted by the church. Father was ordained, an Apostle, elder and high priest before the church was organized, the command of God was authority for so doing, but after the church was organized and the law given, a complyance with the law was necessary to legalize such ordinations.

If this is satisfactory on the points treated Fred I will some time give my views on Reorganization. See?

Give my regards to Josephine, your Mother and the children. I have had the spirit's presence with me in writing this hence I know it is true. Yours in Gospel bonds

Alex Hale Smith

In regard to Bro Whiteheads testimony to Joseph blessing. It was called an ordination in the sense of being set apart to fill Prophelicaly [sic] the office he now fills. The ordination could not be understood to place him immediately in the exorcise [sic] of the office, but when the blessing was confirmed by Wm Marks, it placed him immediately in charge. See?

—Alexander H. Smith, Lamoni, Iowa, June 2, 1897, and Blue Rapids, Kansas, June 5, 1897, Letter to Fred Salisbury, P21, f92, CofC

Alexander and his aunt Katharine Smith Salisbury, 1896.

Quilt top. Handiwork of Katharine Smith Salisbury.

Frederick A. Smith

Alexander sat for a photograph with his son, Frederick A., around 1900. Frederick later filled his father's place as RLDS Presiding Evangelist/Patriarch.

Alexander and Joseph III at a church outing near Lamoni, Iowa, 1900.

Reconciliation

Church of Christ Temple Lot building, 1868-1898. The building burned two years before this revelation. Committee members Richard Hill and George Cole are in this picture,

AROUND THE TURN of the century, leaders of the Church of Christ (Temple Lot), approached the RLDS Church, initiating a series of talks that eventually culminated in a period of functional harmony between the two bodies.

Following a period of earnest and solemn fasting and prayer, Alexander delivered the following revelation to a council composed of six elders of the Church of Christ (Temple Lot), and six elders of the Reorganized Church of Jesus Christ of Latter Day Saints:

Elders of the Church of Christ (Temple Lot): Richard Hill, George P. Frisby, George D. Cole, Alma Owen, John R. Halderman, and Abraham L. Hartley.

Elders of the Reorganized Church: Alex H. Smith, E. L. Kelley, H. C. Smith, Joseph Luff, R. S. Salyards, and Roderick May:

Verily, thus saith the Spirit: My children of the Church of Christ are not sufficiently humble or willing to submit to my will; they still contend against my words, and thus deprive themselves from receiving many of the blessings I have in store for them. Let them cease to contend against my servant Joseph, whom I called to bring forth my church out of obscurity and restore mine ancient order and ordinances, and this he did and was faithful to me; but because of the wickedness of the world, and the falling away of his brethren, and the failure of my children to keep my commandments given through him, I have taken him to myself.

Let my children of the Reorganization of my church, and my children of the Church of Christ, cease to contend one against the other, in the spirit of contention for mastery; but commune one with another in peace and loving kindness; and let my children of the Church of Christ cease to contend against the revelations I have given through my servant, because they do not understand all the things I have given. Behold, I have spoken as seemed good in me, and in mine own time will I make it plain. Behold, it is my will that you become reconciled to thy brethren of the Reorganization of my church, and join with them in the work of building up Zion and the gathering of my people, and the building of my temple, which I will command in mine own time to be built. Be not overly anxious; thy sacrifices I have witnessed, and am well pleased; yet in many things ye have been deceived. It is my will now that my children no longer stand in the way of the progress of my work; neither make thy brother an offender for a word. There are and will be mis-

takes, but they are the mistakes of men; they can not hinder my work, but will cause loss to those who suffer themselves to be deceived thereby. Be wise and obedient, and I will bless thee, and thou shalt in no wise lose thy reward. Amen.

—Alexander H. Smith, Revelation to the Reorganized Church and the Church of Christ (Temple Lot), March, 1900, RLDS General Conference Minutes, 1900; See also Alvin Knisley, *Infallible Proofs* (Independence, MO: Herald Publishing House, 1930), 47-48.

Alexander H. Smith at the RLDS Conference, Independence, Missouri, before 1897.

RLDS Conference, 1901

FOLLOWING THE restoration of the Patriarchate in the RLDS Church, the tradition developed of Alexander, as Presiding Evangelist, opening the RLDS General Conference with prayer.

In 1901, Hawaiian missionary Gilbert Waller, asked the church to "consider the needs of . . . [the Hawaiian] mission." The Conference then instructed Alexander to visit the islands of the sea and Australia.

—Gilbert Waller, "The Field,"
Herald 48, no. 14
(April 3, 1901): 261.

In preparation for his extended trip, Alexander corresponded with Tahitian missionary John W. Peterson.

Lamoni Iowa June 5th 1901
Br. John W. Peterson,
Papeete Tahiti
. . . My plans have been to leave America near the 1st of Aug, but I lately received a letter from Bro. Burton, which informed me that Metuaori could not get off for the Island until June 30th, and would not have time to notify the natives, and give them time to arrange for the contemplated visit. So my last thought was to arrange to leave Frisco about the 1st of Sept, which will give them a couple of months to get ready. I have not received any thing from Bro. Burton since I wrote him to make the plans and I would work to them. As he is to be my guide and interpreter, and is in touch with the natives, and understands the conditions better than I. His understanding of the finance of the natives is much as you report it, and he urged me to give them plenty of time. As you say my visit will be an "event of a life time with them." So I am constrained to think of it in my case. . . . It is not contemplated to visit Australia first. I must make my arrangements to visit the Islands first. It is thought best by the Prescy for me to return from Australia by way of the Suez Canal, and London, and thus visit England, ere my return to America.

Yours very Respectfully in bonds,

Alexander H. Smith

—Alexander H. Smith,
Papeete, Tahiti, Letter to John W. Peterson, June 5, 1901, MS 17756, f5, LDS Church Library.

South Sea Mission

BEFORE ALEXANDER set out for the South Seas in the summer of **1901** he linked up with Joseph III, who was attending the Bushrod Park Reunion, a few miles east of Oakland, California.

Alexander also attended the Sycamore Grove Reunion, near Los Angeles, just before leaving for Tahiti. Alexander and Leon Gould were part of a party of six RLDS missionaries who departed from San Francisco for the islands of the sea on September 10, 1901.

Alexander had the following dream one night while traveling to Tahiti:

I am here reminded of a dream I had on board the steamship *Australia*: I saw in my dream a native, or colored man, with straight hair and smooth face, a tall, broad-shouldered, finely-formed man, dressed in a white shirt or waist, with a colored pareu or hipcloth, which both sexes wear, legs and feet bare. I awoke and the vision still remained with me. I asked the meaning and was told this man represents those islanders. They are Lamanites, and are worthy and entitled to the priesthood. I was glad to receive this evidence, for I had heretofore had some scruples as to ordaining them to the high priest's office. I had never before seen one like the one shown me, but have since, dressed very similarly.

—Alexander H. Smith, dream or vision, 1901, "Reminiscences: Part 7," *Autumn Leaves* 16, no. 5 (May, 1903): 204-5.

Alexander arrived in Tahiti on October 2, 1901, and visited the islands of Tuamotu, Anaa, Makemo, Raroia, and Tonga.

Though initially hesitant, his dream reassured him that "the natives were of Israel, and were entitled to and worthy of the Melchisedec priesthood, and that Metuaore . . . was worthy. . . ." As a result, Alexander ordained a native church member named Metuaore to the office of bishop during the Tahitian conference.

From there, Alexander continued on to Auckland, New Zealand, and Sydney, Australia.

—Alexander H. Smith, Papeete, Tahiti, Letter to Joseph Smith III, November 28, 1901, *Herald* 49, no. 2 (January 8, 1902): 32-33.

Australia

Some members of the Wright Family, Ina second from left in back row.

IN 1902, WHILE IN Australia, Alex met Richard Ellis, the first RLDS baptized in that land. Ellis had been the former leader of the Sydney LDS branch. Alex also ordained Walter Haworth, editor of the Australian church periodical, the *Gospel Standard*, to the office of Seventy.

Alexander traveled throughout Australia visiting branches as well as Charles Wandell's gravesite in Balmain Cemetery at Sydney. Wandell died in 1875 during his mission on behalf of the RLDS Church in Australia.

Before leaving the land down under, Alex visited his daughter Ina Inez Smith Wright. Ina had married Sidney Wright in 1891 and moved onto the Wright farm in New South Wales.

Alexander recalled his reunion with his daughter. The Wrights lived near a little village called Fairview, nearly a day by stage from Wallsend.

Our driver said he knew where Sid Wright lived and would set us down within a half mile of his place; that he lived back away from the road in the bush. Said Mr. Wright had been over to America some time before and brought home an American girl for a wife.

We finally came to a large gate which opened into what appeared to be an immense timber pasture. Just inside the gate a few rods stood a small cabin, uninhabited. Our driver told me I better follow the left-hand road as I got into the bush, as the right-hand was a log road, and I might get lost. He left us and drove off. There we were apparently in an Australian forest, strangers in a strange land, evening coming on, and our past reading about the "bushmen of Australia" did not have a tendency to make us feel at ease. What if our driver had been mistaken? What if he was in league with those same bushman, and left us just where they wanted us? However, as we could not well carry our baggage—all of it, I left Leon to watch while I went in search of my son-in-law's [farm].

I came to the forks of the road and of course took the left-hand road. I thought the half mile was stretching out most awful long and began to wish I had taken the right-hand road when I came to two fence corners and a lane, evidently a log road, which seemed to lead way up into the hills. I started along the lane and had gone perhaps forty rods when I saw to the right a clearing and away across that clearing to the east or southeast I saw a house. I stopped and looked closely,—it looked familiar. I soon recognized my daughter's home, as she had sent me a photo of it before I left America.

I didn't go back around the road. I just slid through the fence and went straight across to the house in the most direct way. As I neared the house I discovered it was inclosed with a picket fence and a lane led up to it, the garden on one side, the paddock on the other.

As I walked up the lane three great dogs came barking out; but as I am not afraid of a dog, as a rule, I kept walking briskly on and spoke to the dogs and they quieted their noise. I was near enough now to hear, and I heard my daughter Ina say to some one, "I wonder what ails the dogs?" Just then I came in sight, as they were on the back porch. Ina saw me and exclaimed, "It's my papa! It's my papa!"

She gave her husband the baby she held in her arms and was soon in the arms of her papa. Sid soon had the buggy hitched up and was off to get Leon and the luggage. After nearly ten years I was with my daughter once more.

. . . For ten days or two weeks I rested and enjoyed the society of my daughter and grand-children. My son-in-law, Bro. Sidney Wright, was busy at his mills—at home evenings and mornings—but I did enjoy my visit to his little home hugely. . . . My son-in-law and several brothers and their father own several thousand acres of bush-land, mostly fenced in and stocked to a limited degree, with cattle. They, too, are girdling the timber land and passing it through the saw-mills and sending it to Sydney, Newcastle, and other points.

—Alexander H. Smith, "Reminiscence: Part 16," *Autumn Leaves* 17, no. 2 (February 1904): 62-63; "Reminiscence: Part 17," *Autumn Leaves* 17, no. 3 (March 1904): 116.

Hawaii

RLDS mission house, Honolulu, Hawaii, built in 1863.

RATHER THAN returning to the United States by continuing to travel west, as was once contemplated, Alexander turned back to the Pacific, intent on ministering in the Society Islands.

Alexander encountered returning LDS missionaries onboard the same ship.

At Pago Pago, several Brighamite elders came on board on their way home from mission labors in the Samoan group of islands. I learned there was a number of branches of the Brighamite faith there. With the returning missionaries was a young native girl, whom the missionaries were taking home to Utah to educate for mission work in the islands. She seemed a nice, well-behaved, ladylike girl, and I hoped she might be well cared for, and not meet the fate so many of those islanders suffer, coming from the warm, moist climate of the islands to the hard, cold winters of the States—pneumonia.

From Pago Pago to Honolulu we had a quiet ride. We had a Catholic bishop on board, who held service in the first cabin on Sunday morning. I could have had service in second cabin in afternoon, but did not feel so moved, and Bro. Kaler was too sick to do so. I supposed our Brighamite elders would improve the opportunity, but was informed that they were afraid I would interfere by asking questions, and they wished to avoid all controversy. I tried several times to draw them out in conversation, but failed. They seemed loth to engage in conversation, so I did not press the matter.

—Alexander H. Smith, "Reminiscence: Part 21," *Autumn Leaves* 17, no. 10 (October 1904): 441-42.

Upon arrival, in Honolulu, Hawaii, on Monday, June 2, 1902, "the first patriarchal blessings of the Reorganized Church were conferred upon some of the members at the home of G. J. Waller."

The *Herald* informed its readers, "On . . . June 10, 1902, Alexander and his secretary, Leon Gould, left . . . for San Francisco. . . . The Patriarch, covered with leis [wreaths of flowers], went on board the steamer amid a feeling of sadness which came over all at the parting." Alexander recalled:

My own experience is fresh in mind as on leaving Honolulu for San Francisco I was literally covered with garlands of flowers. One, about

a yard in length, was a beauty; with the native Hawaiian flag knotted in a bow, on the shoulder, a silk flag, a little beauty two thirds of a yard long. I prize it highly as one of my prettiest souvenirs. The majority of the branch came to the steamer to see us off and secured small boats and hovered round the vessel and sang songs of farewell, as the vessel swung away from the pier, homeward bound.

—Alexander, "Reminiscence: Part 25," *Autumn Leaves* 18, no. 2 (February 1905): 67.

Leon Gould, Gilbert Waller, and Alexander H. Smith, onboard ship at Honolulu, Hawaii.

Family Photograph

A. H. Smith family: Front left: Vida E., Alexander, Elizabeth, Fred A. Back left: Don Alvin, Emma B., Joseph G., Coral C., Arthur M. (missing: Ina and Inez Eva Grace), 1902.

 LEXANDER WAS AGAIN able to spend time at home with his family in Lamoni, Iowa. Two daughters, Ina (in Australia) and Eva (deceased) are absent in this family photograph.

Hospitality

Group of conference visitors at the Smith home in Lamoni, Iowa, early 1900s.
Front center: Elizabeth and Alex, Walter W. Smith (not related, later church historian)
behind Elizabeth.

TRUE TO HIS MOTHER Emma's example, Alexander and Elizabeth continued to extend hospitality to all who came their way. Here they are shown with a group of conference visitors.

Throughout his later years, Alexander enjoyed the high esteem of fellow church members. However, his health was a growing concern. No doubt with the passing years, his back injury, from his fall from a scaffolding, became more severe. He may have also been suffering from progressive congestive heart failure. Late in Alexander's life, his daughter Vida remembered her father's emaciated frame, intense color, and slow and dejected movements.

—"Biography of Patriarch Alexander Hale Smith," (April 1913) 213.

1908 Memorial

Monument Committee, Nauvoo, Illinois, 1908. Front left: Alexander H. Smith, Joseph Smith III, Heman C. Smith, Edmund L. Kelley. Back left: Fred M. Smith, Fred Farr, and Mark H. Siegfried.

THE RLDS CONFERENCE of 1907 authorized the erection of a memorial to the martyrs Joseph and Hyrum Smith. Joseph III, E. L. Kelley, A. H. Smith, and G. P. Lambert, comprising the memorial committee, visited Nauvoo and selected a site. Unfortunately, financial support did not materialize and the memorial was never constructed.

While at Nauvoo, the committee also paid their respects to Emma with a visit to her grave.

Beginning to feel his seventy years of age, Alex vented some of his feelings to a friend, Noah Nephi Cooke.

... Our numbers [in the church] are increasing, and soon we will have no house large enough to accommodate the general conferences. Our church here is too small now, and the church at Independence, is not large enought [sic], we will have to build a new or change our representative system. I am in favor of changing our system. I believe in an

Elders conference, as provided for in the Law.

I am getting tired of the gathering together of a mixed multitude, of members, and priesthood, and calling it a general conference of the ministry of the church. Our assemblies is composed of Tom, Dick, and Harry, Susan, Jane, and Mary. If they are members in good standing is all that is necessary to make them delegates, and if they can bear the expense and pay their own way to conference, they are immediately chosen and sent as representatives, and they may know very little or ab-

solutely nothing of the general necessities, and nature of the work.

Oh well, Noah don't think I am losing faith, I simply see what we [are] tending towards, what we are drifting to.

Just read and consider, and keep your own counsel. I am no grumbler. I expect that I have written enough, it may be too much, so I will stop.

—Alexander H. Smith, Lamoni, Iowa, Letter to Noah Nephi Cooke, January 11, 1908, Smith Papers, P70-1, f9, CofC Archives.

Monument Committee at Emma Smith Bidamon's grave, 1908: (unidentified), Mark H. Siegfried, Joseph Smith III, Heman C. Smith, Edmund L. Kelley, Alex H. Smith, George P. Lambert, (unidentified), Fred Farr.

Alexander's Death

Nauvoo Mansion House bedroom where Alexander died, northwest bedroom at the top of the stairs.

THE FOLLOWING YEAR during a short visit to Nauvoo, in 1909, Alexander unexpectedly died in the Mansion House, August 12, 1909.

Alexander's death was reported in the RLDS Church periodical, the *Saints' Herald*:

He attended the reunion at Bluff Park, and took part with pleasure in all meetings, greeting Saints and old friends with his usual good cheer and genuine delight. Sunday night he preached the closing sermon of the reunion with his usual vigor and was apparently feeling well, and in excellent spirits. Monday he crossed to Nauvoo and visited old acquaintances, expecting to go Tuesday to Burlington, stopping at the mansion, still his property, but occupied by his wife's brother, John Kendall. In the afternoon he complained of feeling unwell, and his niece, Mrs. Ross, brought home remedies to his aid, but he grew worse and continued to grow worse through Tuesday and

Tuesday night. Bro. and Sr. Mark Siegfried adding their attentions to those of the family, and these joined now by the help of Brother Smith's stenographer, Bro. William Dexter.

A physician was called who gave them no hope, and his family was called. His oldest daughter, Mrs. Heman C. Smith, reach[ed] him on the morning of Wednesday, the 11th. She immediately dispatched for her mother. Accompanied by her grandson, Glaud, and daughter, Mrs. Coral Horner, Sister Lizzie reached Nauvoo Friday morning, but found another messenger had gone before, and she must meet the first bitter hours of widowhood in the home of her bridal days. Amid the wreck and ruin left of former happy and beautiful scenes, she looked upon the silent form of one who had never before failed to answer when she called him.

Brother Alexander died at five minutes to eight on the evening of August 12, 1909, after a constant and unceasing struggle with pain and sickness from Monday evening until late Thursday afternoon.

Bro. Lester Haas with his auto brought Bro. George Lambert from Rock Creek to administer on Wednesday, and again Thursday he went for Brother Lambert, but he came only in time to help prepare the body for the journey home, for a great peace had fallen upon him, and rest and coolness where had been struggle and fever and wearing pain.

At six o'clock on Friday, August 13, they placed the casket in the south yard of the mansion and the little band of Saints stood near him, and gave with broken voices a little service of song and Bro. George Lambert offered a prayer full of sympathy and tenderness. The sun was low, almost down, as the ferry boat carried the body and its attending friends over the rippling Mississippi to the Iowa side where they took train for Lamoni.

He leaves a widow, three sons, and four daughters; one son, Don A., and his daughter, Eva Grace, awaited him in the beyond. Fred A. is in his mission field in Oregon. Ina, the second daughter, lives in Australia. Vida, Emma, Joseph, Arthur, and Coral, and their children, and family of Fred A., and the widow of Don A. with six children, and Lamont, the son of Eva Grace, are all present. In addition to these he leaves a brother, our venerated president, Joseph Smith.

—"His Sickness and Death,"
Herald 56, No. 33 (August 18, 1909): 772.

Nauvoo resident, Mark H. Siegfried recalled:

I . . . well remember the long vigil which a few of us kept in this same Mansion House in 1909 over the ebbing life of Alexander Hale Smith, a son of this good woman. In this house he died. From this house a short service was held before his quiet, sleeping body was taken to Lamoni for burial. He lived in this house with his mother for many years; in this house, he lived with the wife of his youth, here some of his children were born; here he died. Only one of his children was present—Vida Elizabeth, wife of Heman C. Smith. A grandson, Glaud A., son of Frederick A. Smith, was there, his secretary, W. R. Dexter, and myself. His family was widely scattered in church work and could not be reached. We did our best to make his last hours as comfortable as possible. It was a quiet, sad, hot August afternoon when the body was removed to Montrose for the last journey of Brother Alexander H. Smith from the house, the place, and the city which he loved.

—Mark H. Siegfried, "Tributes to Church Pioneers," *Herald* 97, no. 17, (April 24, 1950): 405.

Alexander H. Smith, 1900s.

Grave

Rosehill Cemetery, Lamoni, Iowa.

Rosehill Cemetery, Lamoni, Iowa, ca. 1920s.

THE FAMILY BROUGHT Alexander's body back to Lamoni, Iowa, where he was buried in Rose Hill Cemetery, plot 801, grave 3.

Thus ends this recounting of the life of this remarkable man. Acting his part in a purposeful story, Alexander H. Smith unselfishly devoted his life to the realization of a greater good.

To deal with her loss, Alexander's wife, Elizabeth, spent September to October 1909 with her sons Joseph and Arthur and their families in Colorado. Upon her return to Lamoni, Iowa, she expressed thanks through the columns of the church periodical, the *Saints' Herald*, for the many letters of condolence from friends and church members.

Lamoni, Iowa,
November 12, 1909.
Dear Saints and Friends:

I have just returned from Colorado, where I spent the months of September and October visiting my sons, Joseph and Arthur and their families.

I brought with me from there, and find waiting here, many letters; letters that have been coming to me ever since last August, when the terrible blow fell that left me widowed;

letters that speak of a world of comfort and sympathy; letters so kind and beautiful that I want to answer them all, but my sorrow bears hard on me, and not less as time has gone. As yet, I shrink from writing. Be assured of my appreciation and love, and know that your remembrance of me has brought strength and solace.

Someday I may grow more accustomed to this long, silent mission that holds my dear one from me; but now I feel the absence, so intense and silent, too keenly to write much.

Gratefully, hopefully yours,
Elizabeth A. Smith.

—"A Word from Sr. Alexander H. Smith," *Herald* 56, no. 47 (November 24, 1909): 1125.

Poem

AS THE END OF Elizabeth's life neared, Vida sent her sister Ina a postcard bearing a picture of their mother. On the back, Vida inscribed the following poem:

Dear Ina:
Do you mind the little mother,
In the happy days gone by?
Do you recollect the twinkle
in her merry, laughing eye?

And the dark hair—white as
milk now,
How the years pass swiftly by!

Swift and sure and softly footed
But not vainly do they fly.
For they bring a happy meeting.
Then why need we weep or
sigh.
V. E. S.

—Vida Elizabeth Smith, Poem about Elizabeth Smith, ca. 1915, D1821.1, CofC Archives.

Sons and grandchildren of Alexander and Elizabeth. Back left: Arthur M. Smith and his three sons. Right: Joseph G. Smith, ca. 1915, retouched.

Elizabeth Kendall Smith

Elizabeth Agnes Kendall Smith, ca. 1915.

ELIZABETH OUTLIVED Alexander about ten years. Upon her death, June 5, 1919, she was buried next to Alexander, in plot 801, grave 4, Rosehill Cemetery, Lamoni, Iowa.

Obituary

Again are we made sad by the death, on June 6, of Elizabeth A. Smith, the wife of the late presiding patriarch of the church, Alexander Hale Smith. She had been ailing some through the winter, but seemed to be enjoying fairly good health, when she was suddenly taken ill on the night of June 5, and passed away the following morning.

She was born in Marysport, near Liverpool, England, June 16, 1842, as the daughter of Elizabeth and Elder John Kendall. Her widowed mother brought her as a babe to America, and she suffered in those early years the privations of a widow with small children, in a new country, even though among kindly friends and neighbors.

In 1861 she was married to Alexander Hale Smith, at Nauvoo,

Illinois. To them were born nine children, two of whom (Eva and Don Alvin) preceded the parents to the other side, while in 1909 the family suffered the great loss of the husband and father, the patriarch. But prior to that event she had lived the life of sacrifice of missionary's wife for many years. Those who are acquainted with the history of the church, and have read the items from the pen of Brother Alexander will remember how difficult he found it at times to leave home. They will appreciate something of what it meant to the little mother, left alone with her family, for in that age of slow transportation California seemed more remote than the remote parts of the earth to-day.

For several years they made their home in Nauvoo, but shortly after the founding of Lamoni, removed to this vicinity, living on a farm for a time, but later removing to the town of Lamoni, itself, where she continued her efforts as a wife and mother, to do her duty to her family and her church.

After the passing away of her husband, she retained the home place where the family had lived since 1891, and it is there that she passed away. She preferred the independence of her own home, even though each one of her children had established homes of their own.

However, several of them lived near to her, especially her son, Frederick A. Smith, the present presiding patriarch of the church, and her daughter, Sister Vida E. Smith.

She united with the Reorganization in its early days, and was always a humble sincere follower of the Lord. She was of a bright and sunny disposition, and so endeared herself to many. She was a mother, not only to her own immediate family, but to others who needed her help. During the past few years, she made a home for her son, Arthur, and his motherless flock of five children. She had reared one grandson to manhood, and bore the undying love, not only of her children and grandchildren in America and Australia, but of many others who were privileged to know her.

She has finished her work, she has completed her course, and has entered into the rest promised of the Father.

—"Death of Elizabeth Agnes Smith," *Herald* 66, no. 24 (June 11, 1919): 555-56.

The acquisition by the RLDS Church of the Mansion House from Smith's heirs in 1919 helped perpetuate Alexander's rich heritage.

7049653R0

Made in the USA
Lexington, KY
15 October 2010